THE ART OF MICROBLADING MANUAL

TECHNIQUES
DRAWING
COLORS
MARKETING
& MUCH MORE!

THE ART OF MICROBLADING MANUAL

TECHNIQUES
DRAWING
COLORS
MARKETING
& MUCH MORE!

BEAUTY RESEARCH INDUSTRIES

THE ART OF MICROBLADING MANUAL

Written By - Debbie McClellan
Contributed Writer - Kathryn Alexander
Layout Designer - Debbie McClellan, Chris Anton
Graphic Artist - Chris Anton
Chief Editors - Barbara Louisi, Tiffany Lockwood

Acknowledgement

You are truly an inspiration to the industry.
Thank you so much for your picture contributions:

Debbie McClellan
Kathryn Alexander
Sule Loggenberg
CeCe Cervantes
Elizabeth B Smith
Hotaru Ichinose
Alyssa Bingham
Storie Myers
Katrina Childs
Samira Haddad
Sally Choi

Beauty Research Industries
23401 El Toro Rd Suite 101
Lake Forest, CA 92630
Info@BRIManualscom
www.BRIManuals.com
Phone: 949-581-2044

ALSO AVAILABLE *THE PERMANENT MAKEUP MANUAL* **WITH DVD**

Beauty Research Industries produces comprehensive educational books, manuals and DVDs for the beauty industry. Beauty Research Industries will continually update and revise material contained in this manual. If you have any comments or suggestions, please email us.

Second Edition January 2018

Disclaimer:

This manual is intended to be an instructor's class manual or additional educational material for a microblade artist. It is not meant to serve as a standalone guide. Instructional class with a hands on workshop experience is still required.

ISBN-13:978-0-692-95272-6
ISBN-10:0-692-95272-6

Education

Chapter 1
The Art Of Microblading

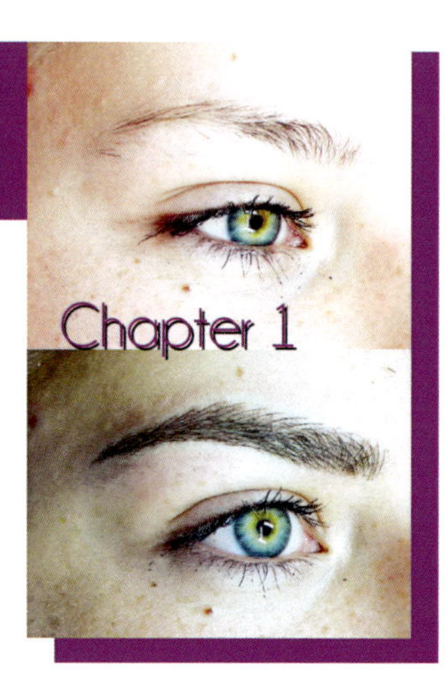

Chapter 2
Infection Prevention & Control Plan

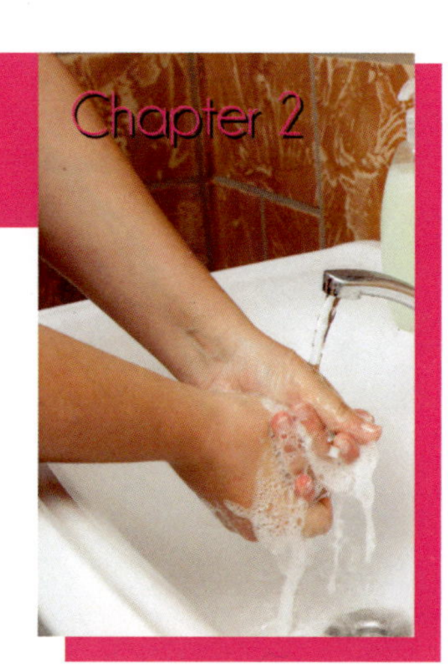

Chapter 3
Skin Anatomy

Chapter 4
Color Theory & The Skin

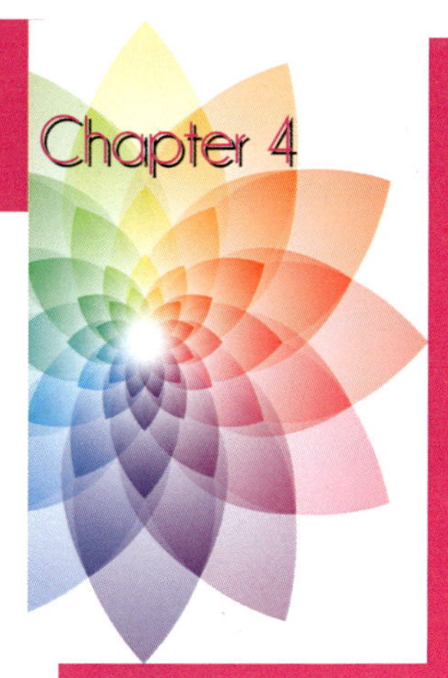

Chapter 5
Drawing Hair Strokes

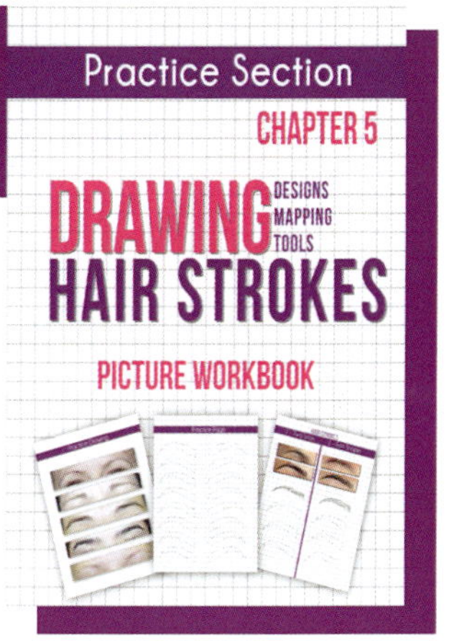

Chapter 6
Implanting Color Techniques

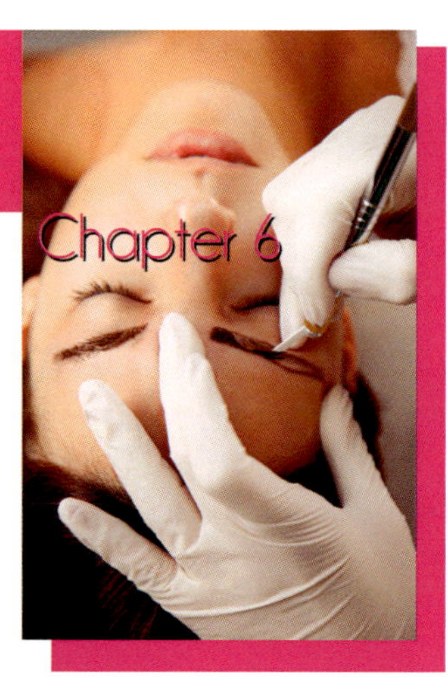

Chapter 7
Steps For A Microblade Procedure

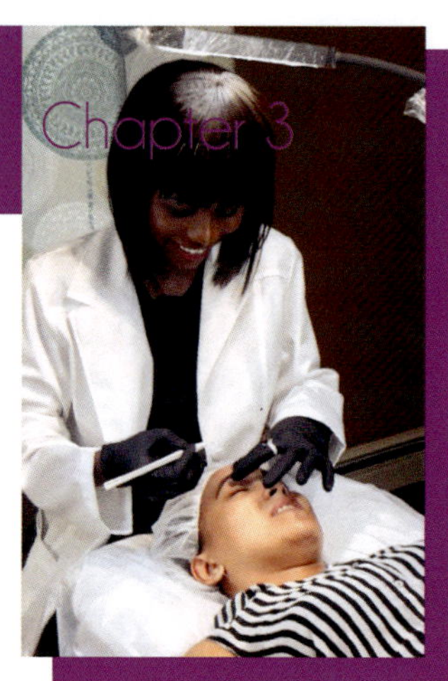

Chapter 8
Marketing Your Business

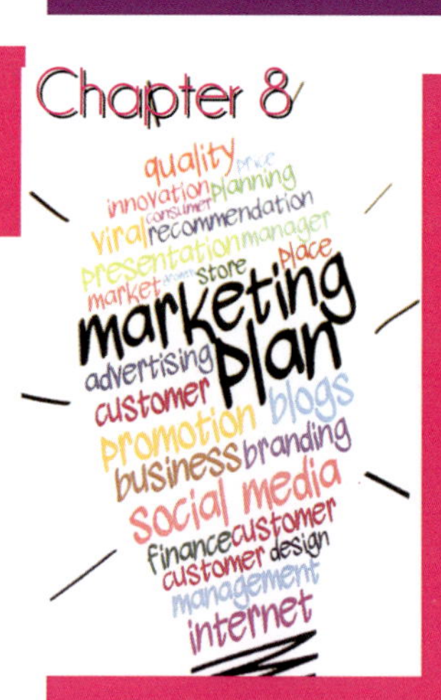

INTRODUCTION

We all love it when something new is introduced into the world of beauty. We have now embraced the natural look of stimulated hair strokes that can make eyebrows look stunningly beautiful. Microblading has opened the doors to new careers for many people around the world. Artists are able to tap into their creativity and enhance eyebrows in a way that women previously have only dreamed about.

Taking on the challenge of becoming a microblade artist has to be taken seriously. This manual is an ongoing guide that can help with everyday questions about safety, color, drawing hair strokes, the different forms for clients, etc.

Every aspect of being a microblade artist must be taken into consideration and practiced diligently. An artist not only must choose the right shape and color for the client, but the depth and placement of the color is paramount. Other factors include whether or not the client is a candidate for the procedure, and knowing the safety precautions to take at all times. When taking on a new career, there is a comfort zone that can only can be acquired through experience.

Chapter 1

THE ART OF MICROBLADING

CHAPTER OUTLINE

- What Is Microblading?
- Who Are Microblade Clients?
- Is Everyone A Candidate For Microblading?
- A Career As A Microblade Artist
- Regulations And Insurance

INTRODUCTION TO MICROBLADING

The latest eyebrow trend sweeping the world of beauty is a highly requested technique called microblading. It can also be referred to as eyebrow embroidering, hair strokes, 3D brows or feather look. This semipermanent eyebrow procedure is created by implanting simulated hair strokes that follow each person's unique pattern of hair growth. Check social media to see how this incredible procedure can make a person's eyebrows look naturally beautiful.

Although microblading is popular today, this tattoo technique dates back centuries. Some cultures would scratch designs into the skin using sharp sticks, wood or stone. Ashes would be rubbed into the cut and the skin would be left to heal, leaving a semipermanent design. Other cultures used finer tools to scratch in designs and patterns using fruits, berries, and other natural objects of color to soak into the skin, leaving colorful designs. Legend has it that Cleopatra used this method to enhance her facial features; Ancient Egyptian microblading at its finest.

What is Microblading?

Microblading is a semipermanent procedure in which color (pigment) is implanted into the skin with a sterile hand tool which holds tiny needles. Most health departments and agencies that regulate cosmetic tattooing consider microblading to be a form of body art tattooing because it involves the use of needles. Microblade Artists must follow all the rules and regulations of their local agency which includes certification for bloodborne pathogens.

With traditional cosmetic tattooing, an artist uses a machine or device to implant color into the deeper dermis layer of the skin. With a microblading procedure, the color is implanted in the shallower layer called the upper dermis layer.

The microblade design tool consists of very fine, small needles aligned in a single-row. They are arranged on either a slanted, sloped or U shaped configuration for producing 'hair stroke effects'. To produce a 'shading effect', a staggered round, flat, or double row needle is used. A variety of special hand tools used in microblading can be purchased to create natural-looking hair strokes.

One of the challenges to being a successful microblade artist is to master eyebrow designs that flow with each client's eyebrow hair growth. Chapter Five will go into depth on the art of drawing hair strokes. It includes a practice section with pictures of real eyebrows and drawing guides that will help with learning the art of basic eyebrow hair stroke designs.

It's important to be able to implant the color into the right layer of skin which is referred to as the "Sweet Spot" or "Target Zone." If the color is implanted correctly, the strokes will heal with optimal results. Chapter Six goes through all the important steps to learning the process of implanting color.

Who are Microblade Clients?

When the eyebrows are shaped with an arch that accents the eyes, it can make a face look beautifully balanced. People of all ages are attracted to having their eyebrows enhanced, especially because the color won't wash off. Women enjoy going from work to evening wear without having to touch up their eyebrows. Some may want a microblade procedure in order to save time from their demanding schedules. Others may want to enhance their appearance simply to make themselves look and feel better. Here are several reasons why microblading is in demand:

- People who have sparse or no eyebrow hair.
- People who participate in sport activities and who do not want to look washed-out after working out, swimming, camping, dancing, exercising, etc.
- Those with busy life styles who don't have time to apply makeup daily.
- People with asymmetrical eyebrows who want to make uneven areas appear balanced.
- Anyone with eyebrow hair loss from prolonged waxing, tweezing, or medical conditions.
- Those who are not artistic in drawing on their eyebrows.
- Anyone struggling with sensitive skin, seasonal allergies, or allergic reactions to conventional makeup.
- People who have difficulty drawing on their eyebrows because of

poor vision without eyeglasses, contact lenses, or vision loss due to eye conditions such as cataracts or Macular Degeneration.

- Anyone with unsteady hands due to muscle weakness, joint pain, or motor skill impairment which makes applying makeup challenging, e.g. Rheumatoid Arthritis, Multiple Sclerosis, stroke survivors, and many other conditions that could cause muscle weakness or unsteadiness.

Is Everyone a Candidate for Microblading?

Before performing a microblade procedure, make sure each client is a good candidate. It is important that prior to a procedure, the artist discuss and provide a written pre-procedure information sheet. The form should include any medical and other pre-existing conditions which may prevent a client from having a procedure. There is a sample of this form on page 21. In some cases, a client may need to check with their doctor before having a procedure done. Here are a few reasons a person may not immediately qualify for a microblade procedure:

- Are currently pregnant.
- Have cancer and are undergoing chemotherapy or radiation.
- Are on Accutane, antibiotics, iron supplements, anticoagulants, etc.
- Have an open wound present.
- Have skin that is extremely thin or severely wrinkled.
- Have a bacterial or viral infection.
- Have a history of keloid hypertrophic scarring.

Another important aspect of performing a microblade procedure is to consider the condition of a person's skin. On one hand, a microblade eyebrow procedure applied with a beautiful arch, can enhance a person's face at any age, but there is a little more to it than that. The canvas on which you are implanting color will determine the final results. Great painters know that the outcome of their work depends greatly on the canvas upon which they are painting. The same concept applies to microblading. The skin you are working on is your canvas.

An oil painter paints on a canvas generally made from either linen or cotton, natural fibers that are woven together either tightly or loosely, and then stretched over a frame. Each fiber comes in different textures or weights. The texture depends on the weave; so a finely woven canvas (younger, healthy skin) is smooth and best suited for small, detailed work. A rough textured canvas, (older or damaged skin), is preferred by painters who use different techniques and brush strokes to achieve the desired result. Similarly, a microblade artist needs to consider that a person with skin that has aged rapidly and/or has been sun damaged, may not be a candidate for a microblade procedure. Extremely thin skin may bleed more, not retain the color well and/or may have a slower healing process.

> It is important that before a procedure, the artist discuss and provide a written pre-procedure information sheet.

How Long Does a Microblade Procedure Last?

There are many factors to consider. Therefore, there is no exact answer to the question of how long each procedure will last. The eyebrows could last a short amount of time or even up to a year or more. It depends on the artist, their ability to implant color in the right layer of skin, and how dark the color was that was chosen for the procedure.

Because the top layers of the epidermis are made up of dead skin or cells that turn over at a fast rate, microblading is called a "semipermanent" procedure. The theory is that as the skin cells shed, the color sheds along with them. This fading of color and cell turnover time is faster than a traditional cosmetic tattoo which implants the color deeper into the skin. The key to microblading is not to implant the color into the top epidermal layers of the skin as the color will fade too quickly. The artist must reach the proper skin layer to achieve longer lasting results. Refer to *Chapter Three Skin Anatomy* for detailed information on the depth of where the color needs to be implanted.

A Career as a Microblade Artist

With the right skills and an eye for style, your prospects for a career in the beauty industry can be as satisfying as the people you pamper, and why shouldn't it be? The beauty industry has been expanding and is projected to continue for many years to come. A microblade artist enriches the beauty of their clients by further enhancing their natural facial features with beautiful eyebrows. With the right attitude and drive, an exciting career can be built in this unique field which can be both lucrative and rewarding.

To be a successful microblade artist, it's important to learn the art of drawing hair strokes and the technique of implanting them with color. This manual has been designed to help the beginner, as well as the experienced microblade artist, obtain relevant information that will offer the quickest path to build an exciting career.

Natural Skills Necessary to be a Microblade Artist

In addition to learning the techniques involved in becoming a microblade artist, the following natural skills are also a necessity:

An Artistic Eye - Learning how to visualize and draw the eyebrows to complement each individual's unique face and features takes a special talent. Eyebrows look natural when the artist draws them to flow with the natural bone structure.

A Steady Hand - Having a steady hand when it comes to performing a microblade procedure is a must. This is for the safety of the client as well as their satisfaction with the final appearance of the procedure itself.

Clear Vision - It is critical to be able to clearly see fine details when performing a microblade procedure. As we age, our vision can begin to decline. It is important to be aware of any changes that occur with one's eyesight and take corrective action, if necessary, e.g. prescription glasses, contact lenses or other available options.

Your Professional Opinion Counts

You are the expert and your clients will look to you for advice. Don't hesitate to offer your opinion. Being able to enhance their eyebrows is what they are expecting from you. This will become evident by the satisfaction you will experience in knowing your client is happy with the end result. It's very important because each client represents your work.

There will be times when a client will ask to have their eyebrows applied in a way you feel does not complement their face. Some may like their eyebrows arched too high, thick or thin for their face. This is where your training and people skills will help in guiding clients. Don't hesitate to let them know that a fashion fad they are infatuated with right now may not be the look they want in the future. Try to educate clients. Explain how you would like to offer your professional opinion. Draw on their eyebrows to provide a visual representation. You want to be proud of your work, so when your clients show off their microbladed eyebrows to all their friends, family and coworkers, you will reap the benefits. Word of mouth is your greatest marketing tool!

The Importance of Before, After and Healed Pictures

Having the right pictures is one of the most important marketing tools. Before, after and healed pictures can be used in a variety of ways. For example, with your client's permission and a signed release form, you can then use their photos in your professional portfolio, marketing brochures, websites, displays, advertisements and social media. Pictures will always impress your potential clients because they help them to visualize the results they can expect. The after picture should be taken at least three weeks following the procedure when the eyebrows are healed. The final results are the most important.

Be careful what you display. Be cautious of using pictures of eyebrows which are too thick, thin or dark, naturally uneven or have healed with a cool grayish hue. Choose the pictures very carefully, and consider what most people will find attractive and natural looking.

Have your client stand in front of a plain wall when you are taking pictures. A camera is essential. Most cell phones can also take close-up, good quality pictures. It's important to take high resolution pictures for certain marketing avenues. Remember, one of the key elements to your success will be determined by the selection of pictures that both represent and glamorize your work.

Touch Ups are Part of the Process

After a microblade procedure, touch ups are common. It is part of the process to add additional hair strokes and darken ones that may have healed too light. Experience and practice increases your ability to implant color so touch ups are minimal. Touch ups are done usually a month after the initial procedure. Many microblade artists charge for touch ups, others include them in the cost of the procedure.

Before you begin a touch up, always re-measure the eyebrows, even if you can see where the procedure was previously done. This will help ensure you implant color evenly.

Rare Allergic Reaction

In extremely rare cases, people have reported an allergic reaction to the colors (pigments) that were used. Check with your insurance company regarding their guidelines and requirements for performing patch tests on each client. If a rare reaction were to occur, it may not show for a long period of time, making the patch test inconclusive.

Also, in rare cases, a person may be allergic to the aftercare antibiotic ointment. It is advisable to add to the aftercare instruction sheet, that if redness or irritation occurs, the first step is to immediately discontinue using the aftercare antibiotic ointment and instead switch to a milder ointment. Prior to a procedure, clients may inform you that they are allergic to latex. Always have non-latex gloves available.

Aftercare is Important

When it comes to microblading, there is a different healing process and aftercare protocol than traditional cosmetic tattooing. With microblading, healing of the skin occurs mainly on the outside of the skin, very much like a minor surface cut or scratch you would encounter while working in the garden. It is the same type of healing which forms a scab or crust. The scab protects the injured skin and flakes off as the skin underneath no longer needs the protection. The color within the controlled injury, or eyebrow stroke, heals inside the skin, creating the illusion of hairs forming the eyebrow shape. Refer to the sample aftercare form on page 23.

Forms for a Microblade Procedure

Counties, states, and countries have different protocols regarding release forms and guidelines. These rules are not only designed to ensure the safety of the client, but the technician as well. Here are a few general information forms you should have on hand:

> **Pre-procedure care and concerns form** should cover any health issues or other concerns a new client should take into consideration before having a microblade procedure done. It should also cover items that should be avoided before a procedure, such as supplements, medications, caffeine, alcohol and activities.
>
> **Consent information form** should be filled out the day of the procedure. It must have a check list of any medical issues or other problems that could interfere with the procedure. It should also include personal information such as address, phone number, etc. The client

must sign that they are consenting to have a microblade procedure performed. Some insurance companies require keeping the consent forms on file for at least ten years.

Aftercare information form should be given to each client at the time of their microblade procedure. The artist needs to confirm that each client understands the aftercare instructions and how to take care of their freshly microbladed eyebrows, including anything necessary to avoid during the healing process.

For copies of generic sample information forms, refer to pages 21 to 23.

After a microblade procedure, touch ups are common. It is part of the process to add additional hair strokes and darken ones that may have healed too light.

Regulations and Insurance

When it comes to performing microblade procedures, guidelines and regulations vary from city, county state, and countries. Always check with the agencies closest to where you plan to work as a microblade artist. There are some health departments that require the artist to register annually for a bloodborne pathogen class and follow an infection prevention and control plan, as seen in chapter two. Various health departments and agencies may have different educational requirements for a microblade artist.

It is essential to have the proper coverage from an insurance company that specializes in providing the microblade artist with professional liability insurance. It is common for insurance companies to charge more if you want to be insured to do any specialized services, such as color removal. There are also building liability policies to protect your place of business if someone were to fall or become injured. Both types of policies usually are offered by the same insurance company.

Important Client Forms

- Pre-Care
- Consent
- Aftercare

Microblade Eyebrow Procedure

Pre-care Instructions & Guidelines for Application

The following are a few issues that will NOT qualify a person for a microblade procedure:

- Is currently pregnant
- Has cancer and are undergoing chemotherapy or radiation
- Steroid Medication and Prednisone (off for at least 2 months)
- Has an open wound present
- Has aged skin that is extremely thin or severely wrinkled
- Has a bacterial or viral infection

Please check with the following with your doctor before having a microblade procedure:

- Have diabetes and under doctor care.
- Have been in remission from cancer for 1 year
- Have high blood pressure
- Using blood thinning prescriptions
- Have seborrheic dermatitis

The following facial procedures must be avoided 4 weeks before the micro-blade procedure:

- No Botox or Chemical Peels of any kind. These include Glycolic, Pumpkin, Alpha Hydroxy Acid, Salicylic Acid, Microdermabrasion, Laser Facials, both ablative and non-ablative. Also included are Fraxel, Co2, and IPL laser treatments

The following procedures must be avoided 1 week prior to a microblade procedure:

- All blood thinners including Ibuprofen, Tylenol, Advil, Aleve, Motrin, Aspirin, Excedrin, Warfarin, Coumadin, Oil Supplements such as Fish Oil, Vitamin E Oil, Primrose Oil
- Antibiotics, Iron Supplements and Magnesium all compromise the integrity of the skin and avoid Retin-A or any strong skin care products
- Any mood-altering drugs

Pre-Procedure Instructions

- Please eat something 20-30 minutes prior to your appointment. This keeps your blood sugar steady and helps you to be more comfortable and less sensitive.
- Avoid any form of caffeine 2-3 hours prior to your appointment. Caffeine is a stimulant and will heighten your sensitivity.
- If you bruise easily, we recommend taking Arnica before procedure and after. Arnica is available at most health food stores.
- If you are required to take antibiotics before dental procedures, please follow the same instructions from your doctor before your procedure.
- No working out or alcohol within 24 hours of the procedure.

Microblade Artist name and information here >>>>

Consent to the Application of a Microblade Procedure

Name____

Address____________________**City**_______________ **State** _____ **Zip** _______

Phone___________________**Cell**_______________ **Work**____________________

Email____

Referred By____

Do you have any of the following conditions?

Allergies	_____	Keloids	_____	Asthma	_______
Scarring	_____	Hepatitis A, B or C	_____	History of Fainting	_______
Eye Problems	_____	Diabetes	_____	Epilepsy	_______
HIV	_____	Autoimmune Disease	_____	Blood Thinners	_______
Skin Problems	_____	Heart Problems	_____		

If yes, explain ____

Are you currently under the care of a physician?	Yes _____	No _____
Physician's Name and Phone: _______________________		
Are you currently taking any medication?	Yes _____	No _____
If yes, please explain _______________________		
Are you allergic to Petroleum, Latex or Nitrile?	Yes _____	No _____
Are you pregnant or nursing?	Yes _____	No _____
I have received an aftercare sheet	Yes _____	No _____
I release my photos for marketing purposes	Yes _____	No _____

- I acknowledge by signing this agreement that I have given the full opportunity to ask any and all questions which I might have about the obtaining of a microblade procedure.
- I acknowledge that I have truthfully represented that I am over the age of eighteen (18) years old, and the following information is true and correct.
- I do not have a medical or skin condition such as but not limited to: acne, scarring (keloid), eczema, psoriasis, moles or sunburn in the area to be tattooed that may interfere with eyebrow procedure.
- I acknowledge that infection is always possible as a result of the obtaining of a tattoo, particularly in the event I do not take proper care of the area of the procedure. I agree to follow all instructions concerning the care of the eyebrows while they are healing.
- I realize that variations in color and design may exist because of my skin type and undertone. I understand that if my skin color is dark, the colors will not appear as bright as they do on light skin.
- I agree to release, forever discharge or hold harmless my Microblade Artist from any and all claims, damages or legal actions arising that are connected to the eyebrow procedure or the healing process or results.
- I have read the Pre-care instructions & guidelines for application form and understand what would not qualify myself from having a microblade procedure done. I have also read the pre-care instructions and I understand them and I have no questions.

This is complete and accurate as to my medical history:

SIGNED ____ **DATE**___________

Aftercare Instructions for a Microblade Procedure

It is important to take the time to read and implement the aftercare instructions for safety and great healing results.

- **Important to keep hands washed:** Keep hands away from the treated area. When applying any ointment or cleaning the treated area hands should be washed for 30 seconds.
- **Do not let the treated area get wet:** Avoid hot tubs, pools, recreational water activities or washing the treated areas. When in the shower, do not get water directly on the face.
- **Do not expose treated area:** It is important for the area of the procedure not to come in contact with sweat, animals, direct shower spray or hot water.
- **During healing process:** Wear hat or visor when in the sun. It is important to keep the sun away from the treated area.
- **Makeup and lotions:** During the healing process, keep all makeup, lotions and exfoliating products away from treated area.
- **Sleeping:** Avoid having your eyebrows touch the pillow. This will help ensure the area treated will not be disturbed or come in contact with anything.
- **Tanning:** Avoid any tanning beds or direct sun.

----INSERT CHOICE OF HEALING METHODS HERE----

Important note for the Microblade Artist: There are both DRY and MOIST healing methods for aftercare that can be recommended to clients. Instructions vary on the artist. Here is an overview:

Dry Healing: It's recommended when using the dry healing method to keep the area dry during the healing process. Ointment should usually not be used during the healing process but some artists suggest to applying very sparely once for the first day or for a couple days. Instructions vary on how to keep the area clean. Some artists recommend using a disinfectant spray the first few days, while others suggest applying cool water on a cotton swab the first couple days. Dry healing is especially popular for those who have oily skin.

Moist Healing: It is recommend when using the moist healing method to sparely apply an antibiotic ointment, Vaseline or A&D (not everyone agrees on each of these aftercare products) for at least the first four days or throughout the healing process. The application is required one to three times a day. Also, the cleaning process for removing the accumulating lymphatic fluids differs, from using a cotton swab every few hours the first day to once a day for the first three days.

Each Microblade training course will have their own portal for the aftercare instructions for their students and what ointments they recommend.

What to expect during healing process and protocol to follow: The area of the procedure will begin to feel dry and chapped. DO NOT touch the area with anything other than the recommended ointment or cotton swabs. DO NOT pick at any flaking skin. You may notice some flaking as the dead skin cells begin to slough off. This is normal and is to be expected. Many clients lose 20-50% of the initial implanted color. Eyebrow color goes through phases and may initially appear lighter, but within three to four weeks more color usually appears.

Long term care: After the procedure has healed, begin an AM/PM regimen. For at least a month, use a hydrating moisturizer that is free of any anti-aging or anti-acne ingredients. Apply a 30 SPF sunscreen to the eyebrows to protect against premature fading.

Touch ups: It is important to follow up with a touch up appointment a month after the procedure. The touch ups are necessary to perfect the eyebrows by making any adjustments, such as darken hair strokes that may have healed too light or adding additional ones where they are needed.

Thank you for choosing myself to be your Microblade Artist. Please let your friends know about your New Beautiful Eyebrows!!!

Chapter 2

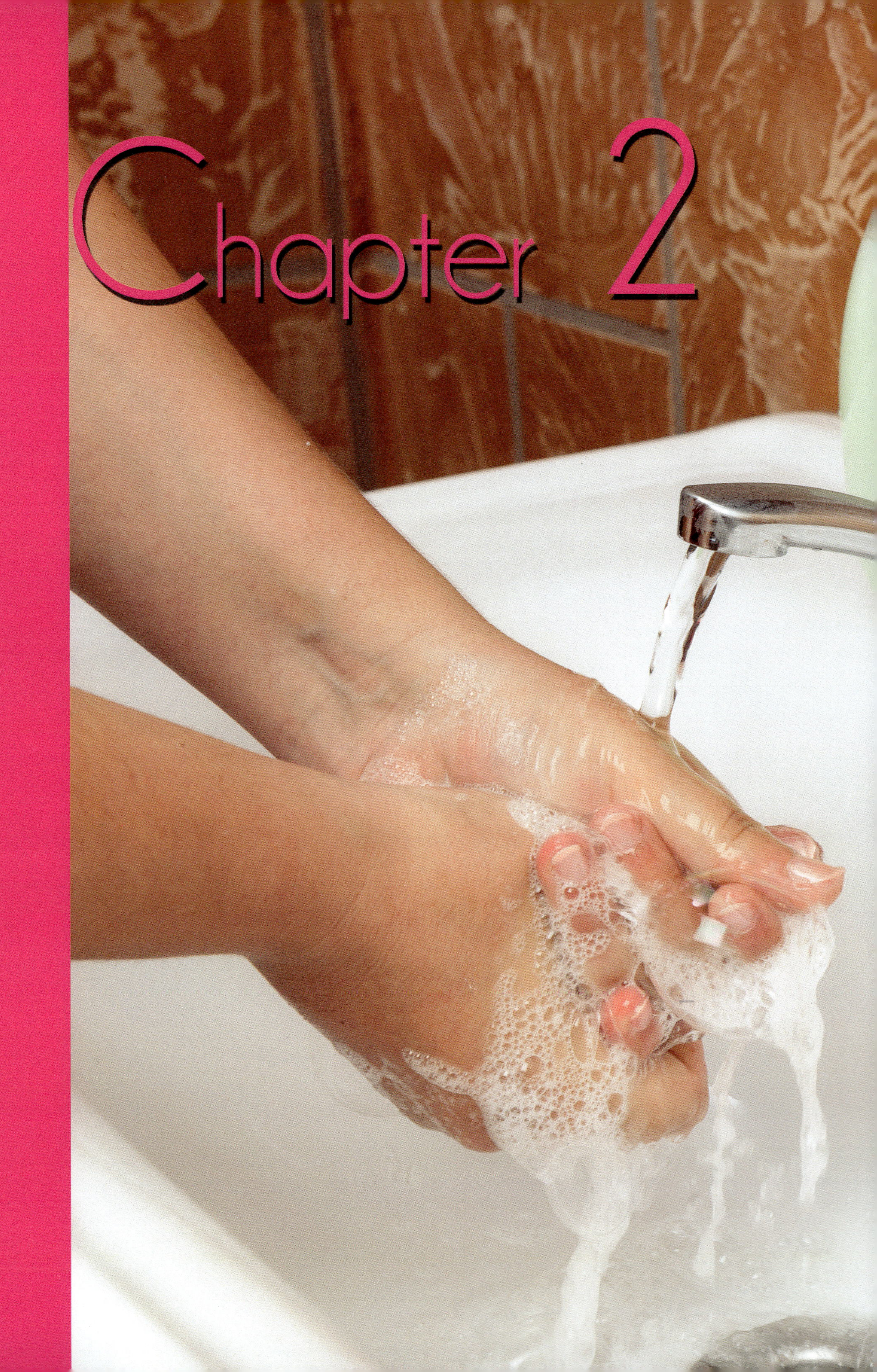

INFECTION PREVENTION & CONTROL PLAN

CHAPTER OUTLINE

- Sanitation
- Records
- Post-Procedure Instructions
- Cross-Contamination
- Setup And Disassemble

INFECTION PREVENTION & CONTROL PLAN

You must have a safe and sterile environment when performing a microblade procedure. It is necessary to take all precautions against any risk of bloodborne pathogens that could occur. Below is a sample of an Infection Prevention and Control Plan:

Sanitation

- Before working on each client and/or if interrupted during a procedure, the hands of the artist should be thoroughly washed and dried using sound hygienic practices.
- Disposable unused examination gloves should be worn on both hands during the microblading process. Gloves should be changed and disposed of into a lined trash container each time they come into contact with an object or surface other than the client's prepared skin or the material being used for the procedure. Gloves should be replaced when they become torn or punctured, or whenever their ability to function as a barrier is compromised.
- Each artist should wear a clean apron, bib or lap pad over clean dry clothing.
- Artists who are experiencing symptoms of diarrhea, vomiting, fever, rash, productive cough, jaundice, draining (or open) skin infections, boils, impetigo or scabies should refrain from a microblade procedure.
- If using single-use disposable razors to shave an area prior to a microblade procedure, the disposable razor must be disposed of in the sharps container after use.
- Only commercially manufactured colors (pigments) should be used.
- Cabinets for the storage of instruments, colors and single use articles should be clean and ready for the artist and need to be maintained in a sanitary manner which protects the instruments from contamination.
- Needles and razors should be discarded into the sharps waste container immediately upon completion of the procedure.
- The surface of all work tables, chairs and benches should be constructed of material which is smooth, nonabsorbent and easily decontaminated with a germicidal solution after each procedure. All

hard surfaces in the procedure area should be disinfected after each client, (according to manufacturer's directions for dilution and contact time), then wiped down with a paper towel which is disposed of into the trash.

- All materials applied to the human skin should be single-use, and disposed of after each use.
- No animals should be permitted in the procedure area.

Work tables/trays and chairs or benches should be decontaminated with a germicidal solution after each procedure.

Records

- Keep records, including signed consent forms, for all microblading procedures.
- A copy of all registrations, licenses and exposure control training for all artists employed or contracted by the facility should be maintained on-site, available for review.

Consent Form

A consent form for each client should be read, completed and signed prior to any procedure being performed.

Post Procedure Instructions

Printed post-procedures with specific instructions on the aftercare of the procedure should be given to each client. Instructions should include restrictions on physical activities such as bathing, recreational water activities, gardening or contact with animals as well as the duration of these restrictions. Signs and symptoms of infection indicate the need to seek medical care.

Sterilization of Needles/Instruments

- Only individual disposable or sterilized needles and tubes should be used for each client.
- Clean instruments and sterilized instrument packs should be placed in clean, dry, labeled containers or stored in a labeled cabinet to protect from dust and moisture.
- Each sterile instrument pack should be evaluated at the time of storage and before its use. If the integrity of the pack is compromised, the package should be discarded or reprocessed before use.

Care of Colors (Pigments)

- In preparing color(s) to be used for a microblade procedure, only commercially available single-use or individual portions of pigments in clean, single-use containers should be used for each client.
- After a procedure, the remaining unused color in the single-use individual containers should be discarded along with the container.

Facilities and Equipment

- There needs to be adequate lighting and ventilation.
- Floors, walls, ceilings and all surfaces should be smooth, durable, free of holes, easily cleanable, and non absorbent.
- The floor of the procedure work room should be made of impervious material. The floor should be swept and wet mopped daily. Floors, walls or ceilings should not be swept or cleaned during a procedure.
- Convenient, clean and sanitary toilet and hand washing facilities should be made accessible to customers.
- The building and equipment should be maintained in a state of good repair at all times. The studio premises should be kept clean, neat, and free of litter and rubbish.

Procedure Area

- Each microblade facility should have a separate procedure area not used for any other purpose. Microblade procedures should only be performed in the designated area.
- All sinks should be maintained in a sanitary manner, and should be equipped with wall-mounted, single use soap and paper towel dispensers.
- Plumbing should be in compliance with the state or local plumbing codes.
- No person should consume any food or drink in the procedure area.

Cross-Contamination

Clients, operators and the community could be at risk if cross-contamination occurs. Cross-contamination issues should be discussed with all artists working at the facility. Some of the ways in which cross-contamination can occur in the procedure area are:

- If one or more operators share the same equipment or materials.
- If clean and used instruments come into contact with one another.

- If clean instruments are placed on unclean surfaces.
- If strict operator hygiene is not observed.
- If contaminated dressings and/or disposable gloves are not disposed of immediately/properly.
- If structural facilities, furnishings and fittings of the premises are not adequately protected, or thoroughly cleaned between clients.
- If towels and other articles used on clients are not changed or thoroughly cleaned between clients.

Operators should be aware of the potential for unprotected surfaces and equipment becoming contaminated with blood during a procedure. Some examples of how this can occur are:

- Adjusting overhead light fittings
- Adjusting settings on power packs
- Answering telephones
- Touching color (pigment) bottles or trays
- Touching curtains, drapes, or bin lids
- Adjusting furniture and equipment

The work area should be properly covered, and all bottles and equipment covered properly to protect from contamination. If during a procedure the work must be stopped for any reason, the procedure site on the client should be covered with gauze or cling wrap. The work area should also be covered with a disposable lap cloth to protect from contamination.

Operators should be aware of the potential for unprotected surfaces and equipment becoming contaminated with blood and serum during a procedure.

Disposal of Waste

A microblade studio operator should dispose of waste products in the following manner:

- Needles, razors or other sharp instruments used for procedures should be segregated from other wastes and placed in a sharps container immediately after use.
- Containers of biohazard wastes should be sent to a facility to be managed as a medical waste.
- Other disposable waste should be placed in a trash container lined with a plastic trash bag.
- Waste containers should be kept closed when not in use.
- Disposable waste should be handled, and disposed of properly and in a timely manner to minimize direct exposure to personnel.

Setup

- Always wash hands with soap and water, and put on new gloves.
- Sanitize the procedure area and all surfaces in which you will come into contact.
- Everything that will be touched or could be touched should be sanitized.
- Remove and dispose of gloves and wash hands up to the elbow with soap and water for a minimum of 15 seconds.
- Place barrier on counter or work surface.
- Put on gloves and set up equipment such as ointment, caps, needles, tubes, pigments, etc.
- Check expiration dates on applicable items.
- Bag any bottles and put barrier film on lamps, controls, arms of chairs and any other surface with which you may come into contact. Put sleeve covers on all clip cords. Once the machine is set up, a bag must cover the machine head.
- Anytime something new is touched outside of the procedure area, gloves must be removed, thrown away and the hand washing process must start over.

Disassemble

- Remove and dispose of gloves. Wash hands for a minimum of 15 seconds with soap and water, and put on new gloves.
- Remove barrier film and throw in trash.
- Take cover off machine(s) and dispose of in trash. Place needles in sharps container. Throw disposable tubes in trash.
- Remove bags from bottles and other containers that are covered and any other potentially contaminated items (including gloves) and dispose of.
- Spray work surface with disinfectant and wipe down.
- Remove gloves and throw away in trash. Wash hands with soap and water.

Chapter 3

SKIN ANATOMY

CHAPTER OUTLINE

- Layer Of Skin To Implant Color
- Epidermis
- Dermis
- Specialized Dermal Cells
- Eyebrow Muscle Anatomy

SKIN ANATOMY

To master the art of microblading, it's important to know the layers of skin and where the color must be implanted. The top 5 layers of the skin are called the epidermis. They consist of shedding dead cells and quickly rejuvenating cells. If the color is placed within these top layers only, the results will last for a limited period of time. Underneath the epidermal layers is the upper part of the dermal layers which is called the papillary dermis. It is also referred to as the dermal-epidermal juncture. It is the goal of the artist to implant color through the epidermis (which is as thin as a piece of paper) and into the papillary dermis referred to as, the "Sweet Spot" or "Target Zone".

Epidermis

The epidermal layers work together to keep the skin healthy. When implanting color with a microblade tool, each layer must be passed through to reach the top dermis layer in order to create a clear "hair stroke look" for the eyebrows.

The thickness of the epidermis varies in different areas of our body's skin. It is the thinnest on the eyelids at .05 mm and the thickest on the palms and soles at 1.5 mm. The epidermis contains 5 layers. From bottom to top the layers are named:

- Stratum basale
- Stratum spinosum
- Stratum granulosum
- Stratum lucidum
- Stratum corneum

The bottom layer, the stratum basale, has cells that are shaped like columns. In this layer the cells divide and push already formed cells into higher layers. As the cells move into the higher layers, they flatten and eventually die. The topmost layer of the epidermis is made up of dead skin cells (which will shed every 3-4 weeks), and are replaced by the lower layer of new cells from below which are gradually pushed upwards. There are three types of specialized cells in the epidermis.

- The melanocyte produces pigment (melanin)
- The Langerhans cell is the frontline defense of the immune system in the skin
- The Merkel cell's function is not clearly known

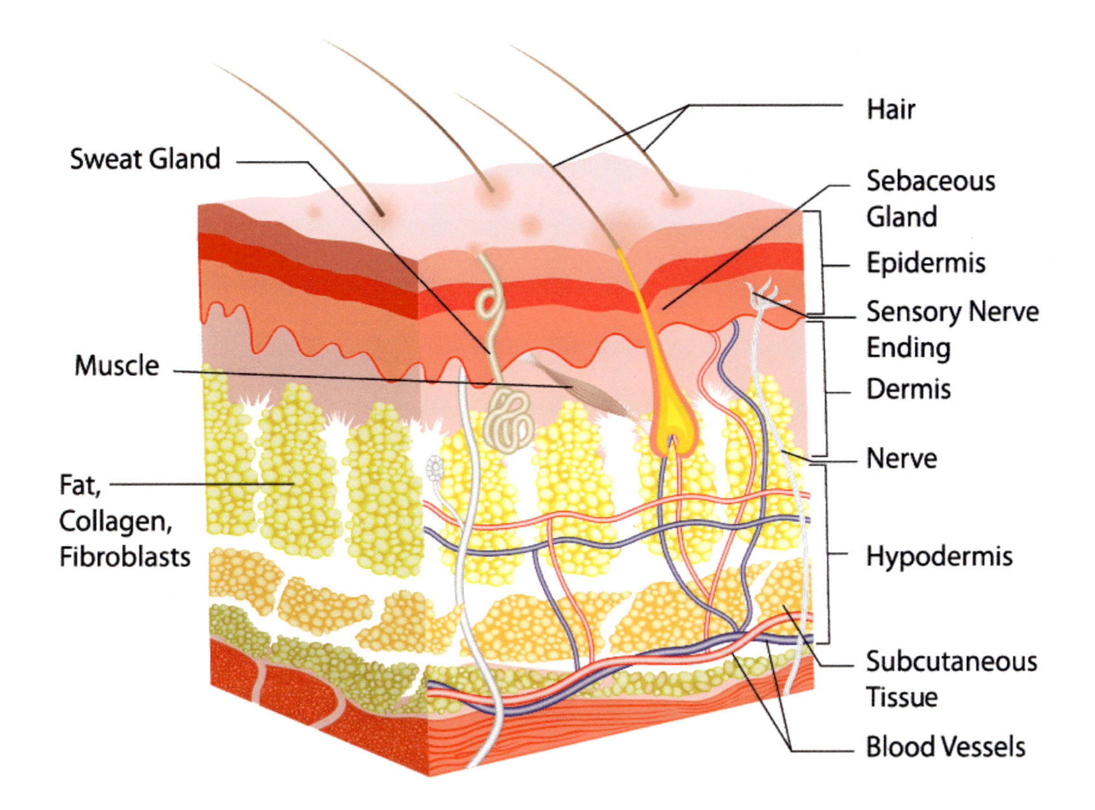

Dermis

The dermis also varies in thickness depending on the location of the skin. It is .30 mm on the eyelid and 3.0 mm on the back. The dermal layers of the skin are a complex tissue framework consisting of our blood vessels, sweat glands, oil glands, nerves, hair follicles and where skin tissues like collagen and elastin are found. The blood vessels carry oxygen to other parts of our body while the oil glands produce sebum which rises to the surface and lubricates the skin. The extensive network of nerves protects us by sending signals to our brain to help us detect pain, temperature, texture and pressure. Collagen and elastin are proteins that help to maintain the skin's firmness and elasticity. The dermis is composed of three types of tissue (collagen, elastic tissue and reticular fibers).

The two layers of the dermis are the papillary and reticular layers.

- The upper, papillary layer, contains a thin arrangement of fibers.
- The lower, reticular layer, is thicker and made of thick collagen fibers that are arranged parallel to the surface of the skin.

Specialized Dermal Cells

The dermis contains many specialized cells and structures.

- The hair follicles are situated here with the arrector pili muscle that attaches to each follicle.
- Sebaceous (oil) glands and apocrine (scent) glands are associated with the follicle.
- This layer also contains arrector (sweat) glands, but they are not associated with hair follicles.
- Blood vessels and nerves course through this layer. The nerves transmit sensations of pain, itch, and temperature.
- There are also specialized nerve cells called Meissner and Vater-Pacini corpuscles that transmit the sensations of touch and pressure.

Eyebrow Muscle Anatomy

The Corrugator Supercilii is a small, narrow, pyramidal muscle close to the eye. It is located at the medial end of the eyebrow, beneath the frontalis and just above orbicularis oculi muscle. Color needs to be implanted on the corrugator supercilii muscle for a microblade eyebrow procedure. It arises from the medial end of the superciliary arch. It's fibers pass upward and laterally between the palpebral, and orbital portions of the orbicularis oculi muscle. They're inserted into the deep surface of the skin, above the middle of the orbital arch.

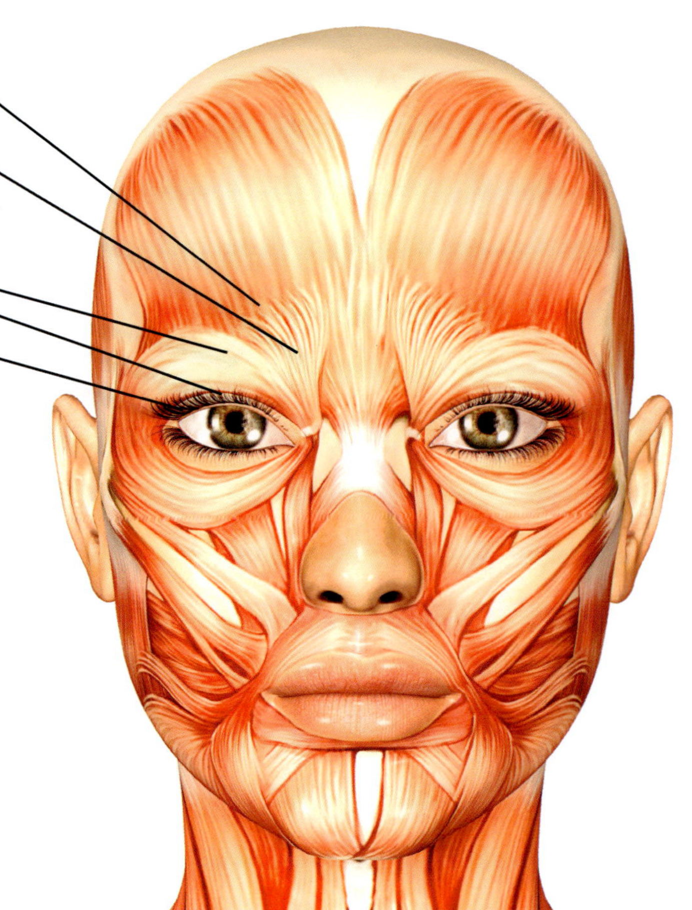

How Aging Effects the Skin

As we age the remarkable functions of the skin that help make it rejuvenate daily slows down, and unfortunately it sometimes almost comes to a complete stop. Therefore a microblade procedure may not always be an option for those with damaged or more severely aged skin as shown in the pictures below.

When we are younger our skin does amazing things to give us that smooth, tight and youthful glow. Within the dermis of the skin the fibroblast activity is in full force producing collagen and elastin. This production of the cells binding moisture and lipid production is at an all-time high. These lipids keep the skin moisturized thereby preventing dry and wrinkled skin. The state of the skin also determines healing times from any injury; minor or major.

The state of the skin also determines how a microblade procedure will heal.

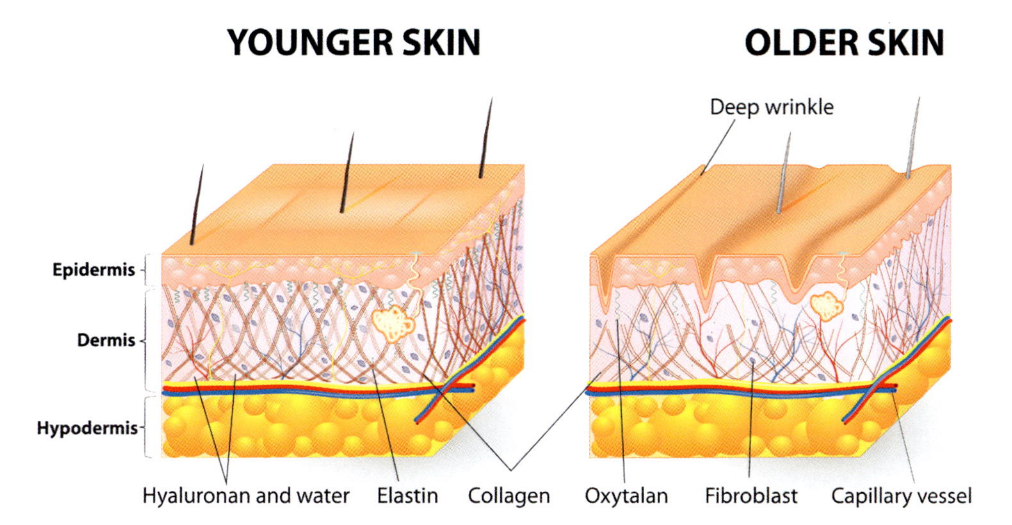

Putting a crisp eyebrow hair stoke into younger client's skin, versus the same stroke into a more mature person's skin is quite different. In the pictures above, you can see that you will get different results. Also, because of the aging process, most mature skin tends to be thin and will bleed very easily which can affect the longevity of the implanted color.

Chapter Sources

Heather Brannon, MD - http://dermatology.about.com/cs/skinanatomy/a/anatomy.htm (Revised 12-19-2014)

Tim Taylor, http://www.innerbody.com/anatomy/muscular/head-neck (revised 2014)

Also referenced 'Just the Facts 101 - Essential Clinical Anatomy by Anne M.R. Aguar, 5th edition

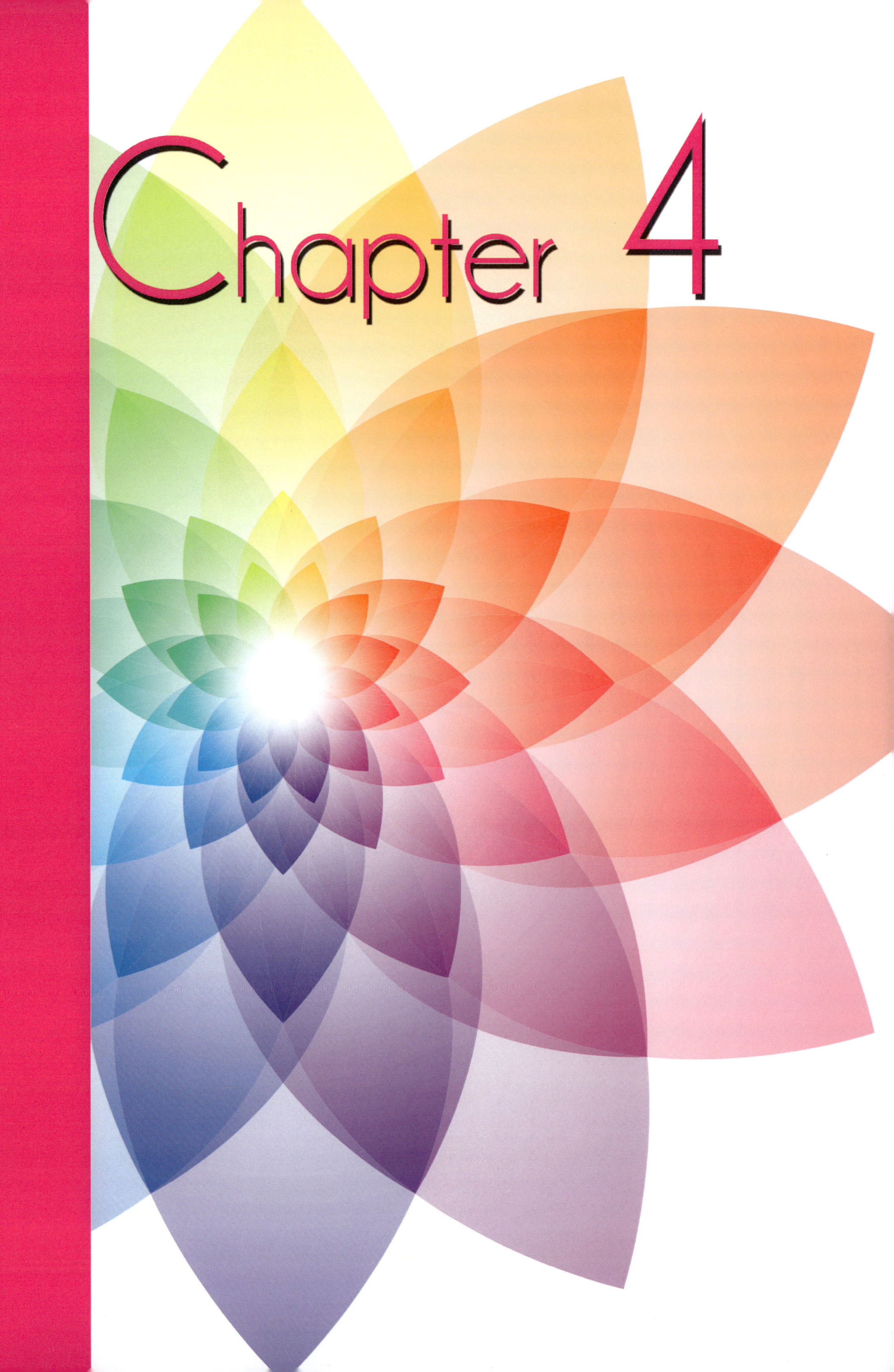

Chapter 4

COLOR THEORY & THE SKIN

CHAPTER OUTLINE

- Understanding How Color Heals In The Skin
- Undertones Versus Skin Tones
- Characteristics Of Cool And Warm Undertones
- Fitzpatrick Skin Type Chart
- Color Theory For Eyebrows

COLOR THEORY AND THE SKIN

As a microblade artist, you will find that basic color theory plays a significant role in the colors that are chosen for each client. Knowing the basic fundamentals of how color heals in the skin and what colors to choose are two of the key elements to becoming successful.

When implanting color on clients' faces, the most important thing is to understand you are not working on a white canvas. The canvas on which you work is the skin. The challenge lies in the ability to determine the canvas color (undertone) and what color to use to achieve the desired results.

Paying close attention, asking the right questions and having a good understanding of undertones, will help when selecting color(s) for your clients. This chapter dips below the immediate surface of the skin and dives into the important concepts of undertones and how they affect the choice of colors. Also, included are picturesof clues to help determine a client's undertone.

It's also important to understand the process of implanting color and why the color you choose makes a difference. If a person's undertone is not considered when choosing a color(s), the desired color may not be the healed result. It is always color plus undertone that equals the healed result.

There are many variations that can affect the final color result of a microblade procedure. With experience and by following a few simple color guidelines in this chapter, you will soon be able to choose just the right color for each client.

Understanding How Color Heals in the Skin

Microblade needles are very fine and can easily penetrate the skin deeper than needed, unintentionally reaching the lower part of the dermis layer of the skin where the undertone can cause colors to heal in unwanted color. To avoid eyebrows healing a grayish color, use a warm color unless a client has a **strong or predominant** cool, red or pink undertone. It's important to use the characteristic charts for warm and cool undertones on pages 42 through 45 to help determine a person's undertone.

Undertones versus Skin Tones

Undertones - Undertone refers to the distinctive color that lies beneath a person's skin which casts color, almost like a shadow, onto the upper layer of the skin. A person's undertone, warm, cool or neutral remains consistent. When choosing a color for a procedure, a person's undertone is what you have to be most concerned with.

Skin Tones - The color of the outer layer of the skin is referred to as skin tone. How much time a person spends in the sun, as well as skin conditions such as rosacea and dark spots, can change the skin tone. Skin tones can range from the lightest pink to the darkest brown. For more information, refer to the *Fitzpatrick Skin Type Chart* on page 46 and 47.

It's important to understand the process of implanting color, and why the color you choose makes a difference.

Skin tones can still play a role in determining the color used for a microblade procedure but not in the same way as undertone. For example, a darker skin toned person or someone who is always tan might request a darker eyebrow color, whereas a lighter skin toned person who rarely tans, may desire a more natural color for their eyebrows.

It is important to note that skin tones, as well as undertones, do influence the appearance of a person's skin but they do not influence each other. This means that both a light skinned (less melanin) and a dark skinned (more melanin) person could have either a warm or cool undertone. Therefore, the color of a person's skin (skin tone) or how well a person tans may not be a good indicator of a person's undertone. For example, an African-American person whose skin tone is darker could have a blue (cool) or a golden red/yellow (warm) undertone; Just as an Asian person whose skin tone is lighter could have a (warm) yellow undertone or a (cool) blue undertone.

Characteristics of Cool and Warm Undertones

There are clues that can help determine a person's undertone. The following pages contain information and pictures showing distinctive characteristics between both warm, and cool undertones. It may be beneficial to cut and laminate these pages and show clients when trying to determine undertones.

Since undertones do matter a great deal when performing microblade procedures, it is important to be well versed in determining undertones. There are a few factors that could help determine a client's undertone. While they may be tricky to detect at first, looking for the right clues can be beneficial. Taking your time to use your best judgment and including your client in the process, sets the stage for choosing just the right color for great results. The following page shows a few basic ways to help determine a warm undertone:

WARM Undertones

In natural light skin can have a yellow, olive or golden yellow cast.

Look best in earth tone colors such as cream, coral, peach, yellow, burnt orange, red-brown, bronze and off white.

Gold jewelry is the most flattering.

Looking at a person's wrist you would see veins that look green, this is because you're seeing their blue veins through a yellow undertone. (yellow + blue = green)

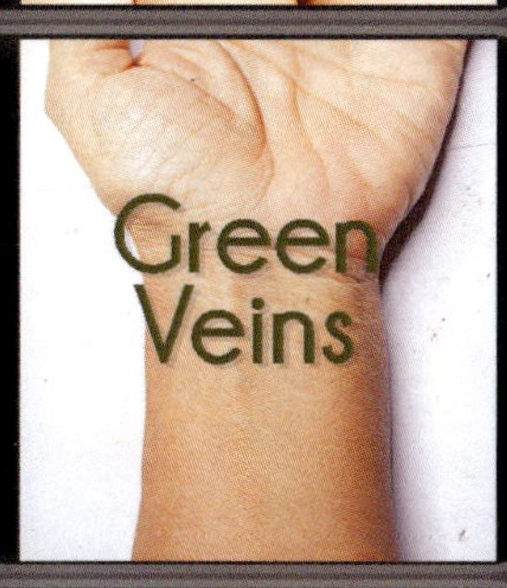

Skin usually tans easily.

When a person dresses and applies makeup according to their undertone, it will accentuate their natural beauty. However, ask ladies what their undertone is, and in many cases they will say they're not sure. What method works best when determining a person's undertone will depend on the individual. It is important to look at the skin in natural lighting. Artificial lighting can be inconclusive. Remember, undertones do not change, so you have to take into consideration sun exposure, rosacea, etc. The following page shows a few ways to help determine a cool undertone:

COOL Undertones

In natural light skin can have a pink, red or blue cast.

Look best in Summer or Winter colors such as: white, blue, pink, deep greens, purples, red blues, emerald greens and black.

Silver jewelry is the most flattering.

Looking at a person's wrist you would see veins that look blue.

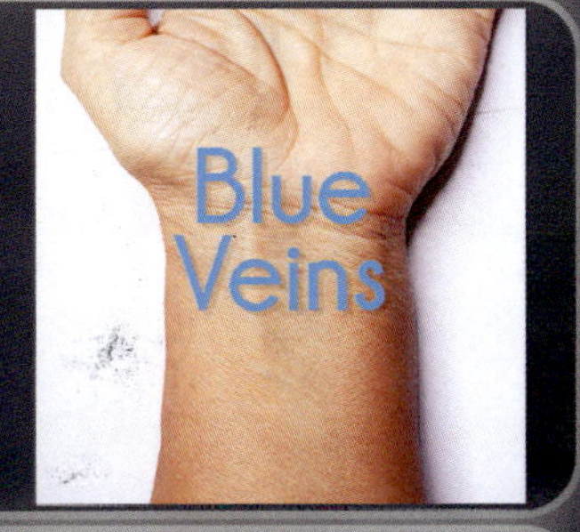

Skin usually burns easily.

Skin Type Chart

The Fitzpatrick Skin Type Chart classifies the response of different skin types to ultraviolet (UV) light and the skin's responses to sun exposure which helps us understand skin types. Thomas B. Fitzpatrick was a dermatologist and the former Chairman of the Department of Dermatology at Harvard University. He created a chart commonly used by the beauty industry to help determine a person's skin type. The Fitzpatrick Skin Type Chart (as seen on the following page) narrows down a person's skin type 1 through 3 (normally lighter skin burning easier in the sun) and 4 through 6 (normally darker skin tans easier.

Fitzpatrick's Skin Type Chart

Type	Characteristics		Photo
Type 1	◆ Pale skin/freckles ◆ Blue eyes ◆ Red or blonde hair	◆ Always burns ◆ Never tans	
Type 2	◆ Fair skin/freckles ◆ Blue or green eyes ◆ Red or blonde hair	◆ Burns easy ◆ Doesn't tan easy	
Type 3	◆ Fair to olive skin ◆ Hazel/blue eyes ◆ Light to dark hair	◆ Doesn't burn easy ◆ Able to tan	
Type 4	◆ Moderate brown skin ◆ Hazel/brown eyes ◆ Dark hair	◆ Rarely burns ◆ Tans easily	
Type 5	◆ Dark brown skin ◆ Dark brown eyes ◆ Darker hair	◆ Rarely burns ◆ Tans easily	
Type 6	◆ Black skin ◆ Dark brown eyes ◆ Darker hair	◆ Never burns ◆ Always tans	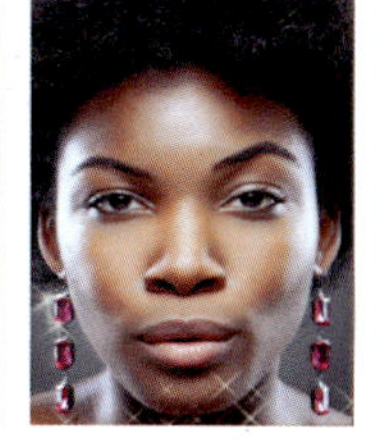

Color Wheel

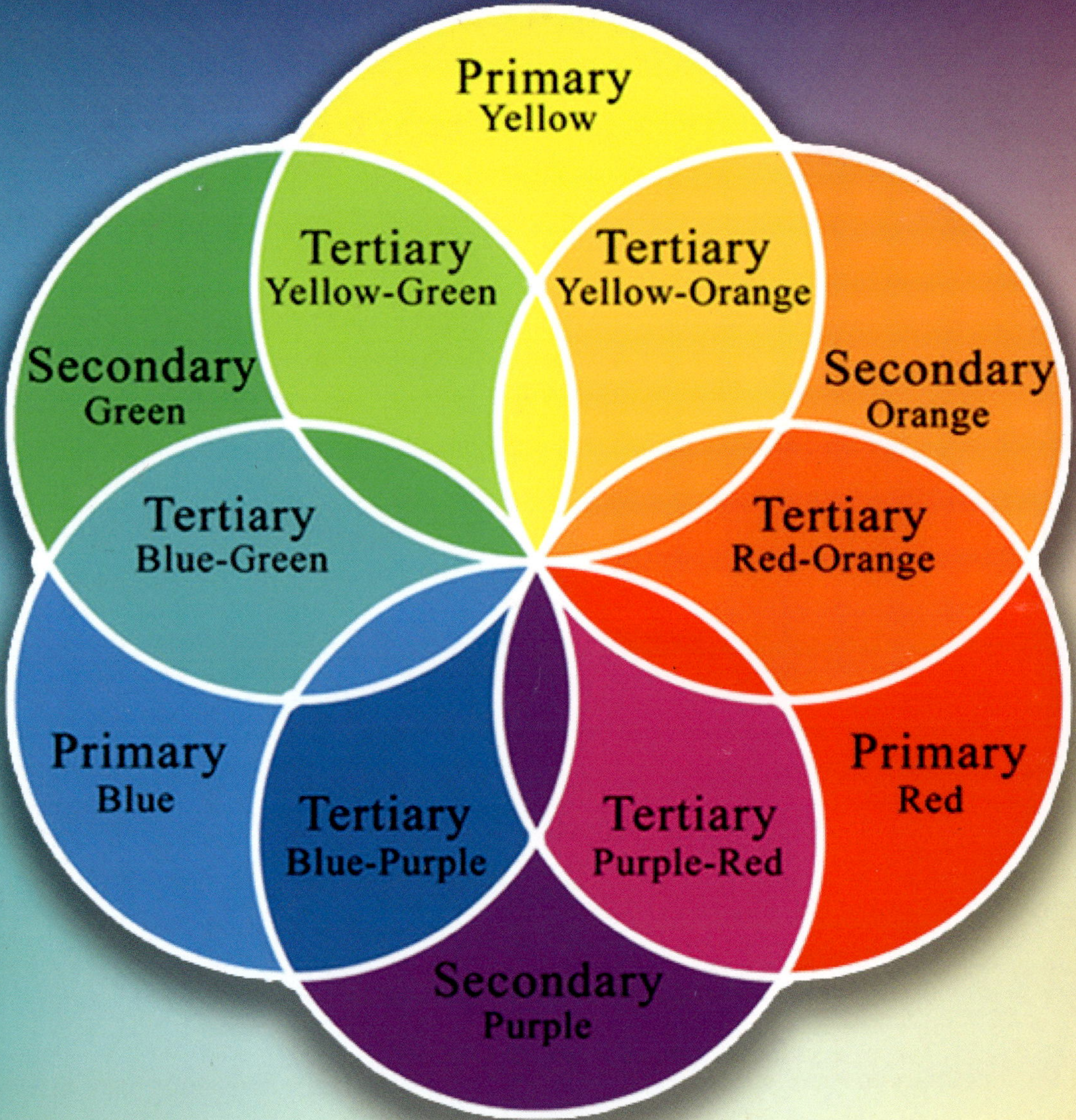

Primary
Yellow

Tertiary
Yellow-Green

Tertiary
Yellow-Orange

Secondary
Green

Secondary
Orange

Tertiary
Blue-Green

Tertiary
Red-Orange

Primary
Blue

Tertiary
Blue-Purple

Tertiary
Purple-Red

Primary
Red

Secondary
Purple

A color wheel is a diagram that illustrates when colors are mixed together, and the variety of beautiful colors that can be made. Generally, Microblade Artists buy colors already pre-mixed, but it's smart to educate yourself on the theory of how colors are mixed. It's a good idea to learn the basics of the color wheel. Being knowledgeable about colors will guide you through the process of mixing and correcting colors. if needed. As you can see in the color illustration above, the main colors make new exciting colors. This is done by mixing Primary, Secondary or Tertiary colors together to make the following colors:

Complementary Colors are red and green, blue and orange and purple and yellow. These are the colors directly across from each other on the color wheel. They're called complementary colors because when seen next to each other they become extremely vibrant and have heavy contrast. These are colors you'll need to know when neutralizing (or correcting) a color.

Analogous Colors are red and orange, blue and green, etc. These are colors right next to each other on the color wheel. They usually match extremely well, but they also create almost no contrast.

Warm Colors are red, yellow, and orange. These colors evoke warmth because they remind us of things like the sun or fire.

Cool Colors are blue, green, and purple (violet). These colors evoke a cool feeling because they remind us of things like water or grass.

Neutral Colors are gray and brown. These aren't on most color wheels, but they're considered neutral because they don't contrast with much of anything. They're dull and uneventful.

Value refers to the amount of black in a color. The more black a color has, the darker its value.

Brightness refers to the amount of white in a color. The more white a color has, the brighter it is.

Saturation refers to the amount of a color used. When a color is at full saturation, it is extremely vibrant. When a color is "desaturated," a large amount of color has been removed. Desaturated colors are close to being neutral because there is so much gray in them.

Shades are mixtures of a hue and black.

Hue refers to a pure color; one without tint or shade.

Tints are mixtures of a hue and white.

Tones are mixtures of a hue and its complement or grays.

Final Color Result and Client Records

There are many factors that can determine the final color result, as covered in this manual. However, there are a few more things to consider as well. Some medications, the PH of a person's body or a person's diet and overall health can even make a difference in the final color result.

Keeping notes of the color and different variations that could contribute to the final color result for each client will give you a better understanding of which colors to select for future procedures.

It is important to have a system for keeping accurate client records. Document the color(s) used on each client by the lot number and date on the side of each bottle. If there is ever a problem, the manufacturer will require this information. When clients return for a touch up or to have their eyebrows freshened, you must be able to review your records to determine the exact formula used.

Mixing Colors

Do not mix colors (pigments) from different companies together. If there were ever to be a problem, you would not know what company needed to address the issue. Also, different ingredients may not work well together.

Most manufacturers of quality colors will allow an artist to mix the colors to get the perfect blend for each client, but it is always a good idea to check the manufacturer's recommended use of their colors.

Camouflaging Unwanted Color

There are times you may be asked to correct a color that was incorrectly implanted, or if a client was dissatisfied with their color result. Trying to cover an eyebrow color is not always easy, particularly if you are trying to match a person's skin. Use caution when utilizing camouflage colors. They can appear brighter, and it can be difficult to match a person's skin well enough for client approval. You also have the choice to turn down a client who has had an unwanted color result or shape from another artist. Most importantly, take your time. Be sure you have the proper training in order to minimize the chance of having to correct your own work.

Choosing Colors

When it comes to selecting an eyebrow color, clients are not usually all over the spectrum. Even our beautiful celebrities know that the right color is important, the basic brown is the most popular. Overall, it can be fairly easy to help most clients choose just the right color for their eyebrows without having to stock numerous colors. Also, by mixing colors, you are able to control the shade of the color, giving you more variety. The following pages will help in selecting just the right color(s) for each client's request and undertone, It also includes a selection of colors that are important to keep on hand.

Color Theory for Eyebrows

When choosing an eyebrow color, a person's undertone can make a significant difference. It's important to explain to each client that you are not working on a white canvas and that it's necessary to take undertones into careful consideration. It is always color, plus undertone, that equals the final color result. For example if a cool color is used on a person that has a warm yellow or olive undertone the color result could be an unwanted grayish color.

After reviewing the undertones characteristics on pages 42 through 45 and an undertone has been determined, choose one of the following eyebrow colors with the correct undertone.

Brown Color Eyebrows

Cool Undertones

Pink or Red Undertone - When a client with a cool, pink or red undertone requests a brown color, use a cool brown with a yellow base. This color will help avoid an unwanted red color result.

Blue Undertone - When a client with a blue undertone requests a brown color, use either a warm brown or a neutral brown with a warm modifier. These colors will help avoid an unwanted grayish color result.

Warm Undertones

Yellow or Olive Undertone - When a client with a warm yellow or olive undertone requests a brown color, use either a warm brown or a neutral brown with a with a warm modifier. These colors will help avoid an unwanted grayish color result.

Golden Red Undertone - When a client with a warm golden red undertone requests a brown color, use a cool brown with a yellow base. This color will help avoid an unwanted red color result.

Neutral Undertones

A neutral undertone is for a person who does not have a predominately cool or warm undertone. An olive undertone is often considered to be a neutral undertone because it is a mixture of colors. To help you choose a color, use the undertone characteristic color charts on page 42 through 45. It can help in determining if a person's neutral undertone is more on the cool or warm side.

Let your client know that if their undertone is different from what was determined, and if there is an unwanted color result, it can be corrected at the time of a touch up and notes will be documented for future reference.

Red Color Eyebrows

When a red eyebrow color is requested, clients with warm yellow or olive undertones have the best results. A red brown color will help avoid an unwanted cool grayish color result.

Taupe Color Eyebrows

A taupe color look best on a person who have ash brown or gray hair. When a taupe color is requested, clients with a pink or red undertone have the best results. A taupe color will help avoid an unwanted red color result.

Unwanted Eyebrow Colors

Gray Eyebrows - An option to help correct gray eyebrows is to use a warm red brown (be careful not to use too red of a color, it may heal too red), or a neutral brown mixed with a warm modifier.

Red Eyebrows - An option to help correct red eyebrows is to use a cool brown color.

Overview

Undertones	Color Used for Brown Eyebrows	Correction
(Warm) yellow or olive, (Cool) blue	Warm brown with a hint of red or neutral brown with a small amount of a warm modifier	Unwanted gray eyebrows use a red brown color or neutral brown with a warm modifier
(Cool) pinkish-red, (Warm) golden red	Cool brown color	Unwanted red eyebrows use a cool brown

WARM COLORS

Warm colors are the most popular for a microblade procedure. They will help prevent colors from healing a cool, grayish color.

Warm Light Brown can be used to help lighten darker colors. It's used when a lighter color is requested, but is usually too light to use alone. Warm light brown is for a person with a warm, olive or yellow undertone.

Warm Brown is a popular color. When mixed with warm darker brown, it makes a desirable rich color. If needed, add a neutral brown to make the color less red. This color can be used with a red brown color, or a warm modifier to help correct eyebrows that have healed, or over time turned to a cool grayish color. Warm brown is for a person with a warm, olive or yellow undertone.

Warm Dark Brown is a popular color that is requested when a person wants darker eyebrows. It can also add depth and darken lighter colors. Warm dark brown is for a person with a warm, olive or yellow, undertone.

Warm Red Brown is for a person who requests a reddish brown color for their eyebrows. It can also be used to warm-up other colors. When mixed with a neutral brown, it can be used to help correct eyebrows that have healed, or over time turned to a cool grayish color. Warm red brown is for a person with a warm, olive or yellow undertone.

#1 Modifier

Golden Modifier is a warm color which can be added to light colors to help prevent eyebrows from healing a cool grayish color. When added to warm color, it can be used to help correct lighter color eyebrows that have healed, or over time turned to a cool grayish color. Golden modifier is for a person with a warm, olive or yellow undertone.

#2 Modifier

Pumpkin modifier is a warm color which can be added to dark colors to help prevent eyebrows from healing a cool grayish color. When mixed with a warm color, it can be used to help correct darker color eyebrows that have healed, or over time turned to a cool grayish color. Pumpkin modifier is for a person with a warm, olive or yellow undertone.

COOL COLORS

Learn to mix different colors to make shades from light to dark in order to accommodate each client's needs. You will find some of the colors mentioned are sold by different names.

Cool Light Brown can be used to help to lighten colors. It's used when a lighter color is requested, but is usually too light to use alone. Cool light brown is for a person with a cool, red or pink undertone.

Cool Brown is a cool color that's used only when a client has a strong red or pink undertone. This color can be used to help correct eyebrows that have healed, or over time turned to a reddish color. Cool brown is for a person with a cool, red or pink undertone.

Cool Taupe is a color that is usually requested when the client has ash brown or gray hair. It can be used to help correct eyebrows that have healed, or over time turned to a reddish color. Taupe is for a person with a cool, red or pink undertone.

Cool Black is usually for a client who has black hair and wants a dramatic look to their eyebrows. Black is for a person with a cool, red or pink undertone.

Neutral Brown is not a predominately cool or warm color. It's a color used for a person who does not have a distinctive, or strong yellow, olive or red undertone. It's a popular color that a modifier can be added to, or it can be mixed with a red brown color when less red is needed.

The following practice section pages can be drawn on with a pen or pencil. You may want to turn the manual around, which is how some artist work on clients. The pages with practice eyebrow pictures, use white-out to cover any of the area that you would want to tweeze so you can see the shape that you're trying to achieve.

Practice Section

CHAPTER 5

DRAWING
DESIGNS
MAPPING
TOOLS

HAIR STROKES

PICTURE WORKBOOK

DRAWING HAIR STROKES

Mircoblading has taken on a whole new art on how eyebrows can be enhanced. Adding simulated hair strokes of color can give women a new look to their eyebrows that they could have only dreamed about. There's is an art to being able to apply this unique, natural look to the eyebrows.

A famous makeup artist in Hollywood once said the eyebrows can appear to give the face lift when enhanced. Most people would agree that eyebrows can make the most dramatic difference in complementing the whole face. They play a vital role in creating facial symmetry. With microblading, concerns such as sparse, thin or uneven eyebrows can be addressed without compromising a natural look.

Shape, fullness and definition of the eyebrows can frame, add balance and give a youthful and uplifted look. This chapter contains detailed step-by-step instructions that will assist the artist in using their creativity and applying it to create beautiful eyebrows with hair strokes. A microblade artist should be able to offer advice to each client regarding eyebrow style and shape that will be most flattering on them. In this chapter you will learn the art of measuring and how to draw basic hair strokes. You'll also be able to practice by drawing on pictures of real eyebrows.

Improving Eyebrows

Eyebrows that flow with the natural bone structure balance the face. There are many people whose beautifully shaped eyebrows frame their face perfectly, and inspire women to take the extra steps to enhance their own eyebrows. A microblade artist needs to take into consideration each person's unique eyebrows. There are many different reasons people want to enhance their eyebrows, from being too busy to apply their makeup every day, to just wanting their eyebrows shaped better.

Here are more examples why women, or men, may want to enhance their eyebrows:

- Improve the arch
- Eyebrows are too thin
- Sparse eyebrows
- Alopecia
- Uneven eyebrows
- Over-tweezed
- Patchy
- Too Short
- No Eyebrows
- No Shape
- Lift the ends

One of the most common mistakes made when enhancing the eyebrows is not taking both eyebrows into account. Many people have one eyebrow naturally higher than the other. In a case where one eyebrow is higher, draw slightly more on the top of the lower eyebrow and under the higher eyebrow. If necessary, and with the client's permission, tweeze the eyebrows to make them appear more even. If you're giving clients a new look for their eyebrows, allow extra time for them to look in the mirror to see if they will be able to adapt to their new look. You want a satisfied client who will tell their friends, relatives and co-workers about the professional microblade artist, who took the time needed to enhance their eyebrows.

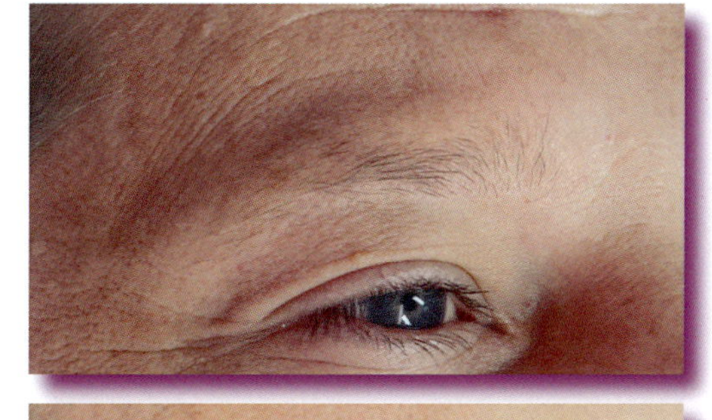

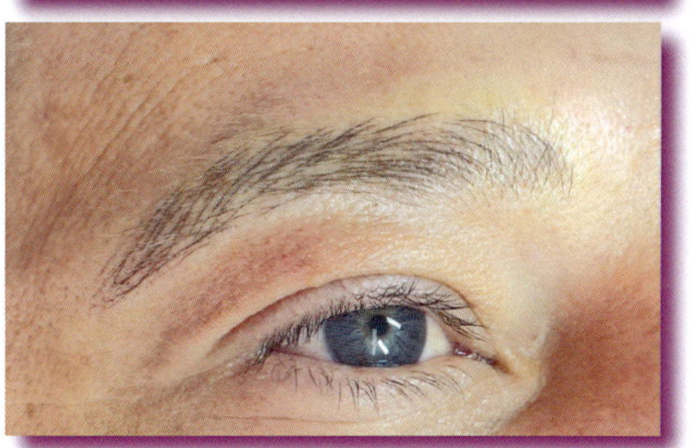

Men's Eyebrows

Men are looking to enhance their eyebrows for many of the same reasons women do. Naturally sparse or uneven eyebrows have men seeking out the natural look that a microblade procedure can give them. Eyebrows that are enhanced can look aesthetically pleasing on men, but is different from drawing on a women's eyebrows. A man's eyebrows have a more natural look, usually without a defined shape or higher arch that women's can have.

Mapping the Eyebrows

There is a measuring process called mapping that will help guide you in making the eyebrows as even as possible. Each person's measuring points is different, depending how their eyebrows flow with their bone structure. Taking the time to map the eyebrows can give you an overall view of where to place guidelines to help achieve even eyebrows. The following page demonstrates the important six points to make the eyebrows symmetrical. Practice page is also included.

Mapping

Step 1

Start Eyebrows at the Crown

For a softer look, measure from the outside corner of the nostril, bringing the line up to the crown of the eyebrow. For a more dramatic look, bring, the eyebrows in torward the nose by adding a few more hair strokes.

Step 2

Arch of the Eyebrows

The highest point of the eyebrow is the arch which is about 2/3 in from the crown. The tail is usually 1/3 of the eyebrow. To find where the natural arch flows, measure straight up from the outside of the iris. On a person with a higher forehead, the arch can be more enhanced. For as person with a lower hairline, a softer arch looks more natural.

Step 3

Outer Length Eyebrows

Begin measuring the end of the eyebrow tail from the outside corner of the nose and eye, following through toward the temple. Women who want a softer look may request shorter eyebrows. For those who desire a more dramatic look, the eyebrow tails are brought out longer.

Step 4

Center of the Eyebrows

Measure the center of both eyebrows by placing a line from the middle of the cupid's bow on the lips, straight up along the middle of the nose to the midpoint of both eyebrows.

Step 5

Top of the Eyebrows

Measure across top of the eyebrows with a straight line, placing it above both aches. This will help achieve the perfect balance needed to ensure symmetrical eyebrows.

Step 6

Lower Part of the Eyebrows

Both eyebrows also need to be measured horizontally, across the bottom using a straight measuring tool, measure across at the lowest part of the eyebrows, to ensure perfect balance.

Practice

Leaning to Draw and Measure Eyebrows

The drawing aspect of a microblade procedure is different than how a makeup artist draws a person's eyebrows. Applying lines that resemble hair strokes to make beautiful, natural looking eyebrows is unique in itself. Here are a couple different ways to show clients the shape and where the hair strokes will be.

- Fill it in with an eyebrow pencil to show the shape of where the hair strokes will be implanted.
- Only outline shape of the eyebrow where the hair strokes will be implanted.

Before beginning the procedure, it's very important to properly measure and take the extra steps to ensure the eyebrows you have drawn are as even as possible. Some artists measure while the client is sitting, others while the client is lying down.

When drawing and mapping eyebrows, stand back, take your time, and use your artistic eye. Consider the shape of the face, including the natural eyebrow bone structure. Determine where the eyebrows would flow nicely. Mapping of the eyebrows, as seen on page 60, will ensure you are able to make them as even as possible. People always have a place where their eyebrows look most natural.

Most clients have an idea of what they want. Ask what they would like to achieve by having a microblade procedure. Do they want more of an arch or fuller eyebrows with more hair strokes, etc. Taking the extra steps to measure, making sure the eyebrows are even before you begin, will save you from having to make adjustments toward the end of the procedure. Once you have your client's approval on the eyebrows, do a final measuring.

Three Point Caliper - As seen in the picture above, the caliper uses three measuring points you can duplicate, by moving the tool to the other brow.
Flexible or Sticker Rulers - There are also flexible, and disposable sticker rulers available that you can use right on the forehead to mark and measure the eyebrows for symmetry.
Caliper - This is a common measuring tool. It has two small movable, manual tension arms to measure distance between different points of the eyebrows.
Shaping Tool - This handy tool has two arms called prongs which can be extended out to measure the eyebrows, making sure they are symmetrical.

After the client has given approval on the shape of their eyebrows and how they were measured, the next step is to outline them with a skin-safe marker. This is important to ensure the design does not wipe off before you have a base to work from. Refer to *Chapter 7 Steps for a Microblade Eyebrow Procedure* on the different ways to outline the eyebrows before a procedure.

Eyebrow Shapes

S-Shaped		
Hard Angled	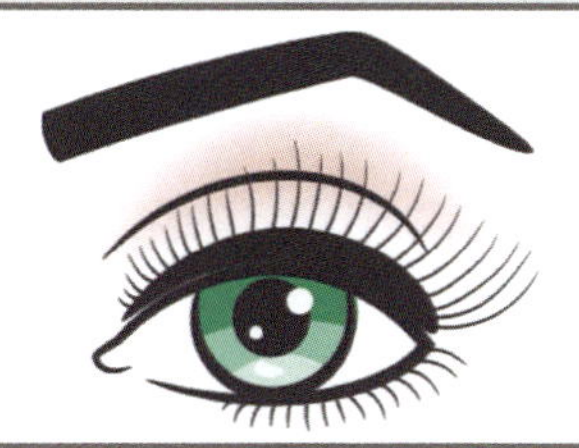	
Soft Angled		
Straight	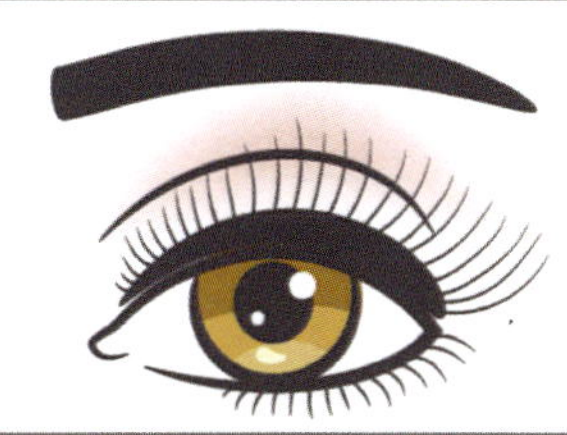	
Rounded	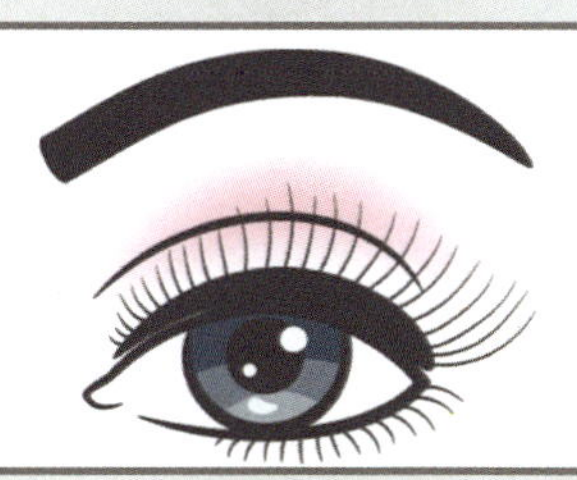	

Learning the Art of Designing Eyebrow Hair Strokes

When implanting color, you're actually placing the hair strokes in a pattern that matches each client's unique eyebrows. In some cases, if the person does not have eyebrows, you will be designing them from scratch. To be successful, you must learn the proper technique to accomplish a natural look. This starts with being able to draw the different hair stroke designs to satisfy each client's eyebrow needs. Observe how a person's eyebrow hair grows, then decide what direction the hair strokes should be placed. As shown in the picture, eyebrows are drawn on, and then with a pattern in mind, hair strokes are implanted in that shape. On the following pages you will learn some of the basic hair stroke designs along with a hands-on practice section.

Face Shapes for Eyebrows

You can generally see where eyebrows flow naturally. However, when looking at the eyebrows with an artistic eye, and seeing something is out of balance, you may have to consider the shape of your client's face. The following page has an illustration that shows common face shapes and how to enhance the eyebrows accordingly.

Eyebrows by Face Shapes

Face Shape		Objective	Eyebrow Shaping
	**Oval** Tapers towards the chin	To maintain its general appearance	Soften the angle of the eyebrows
	**Heart** Has a pointed chin	To balance the pronounced chin	Soften the arch and add length to the end of the eyebrows
	**Long** Long from the chin to the forehead	Break up the face, to make it appear shorter and avoid elongation	Downplay the arch by softening it
	**Round** The length and width are close to the same	Give the illusion of a longer face	Accent the arch and taper the ends
	**Diamond** Noticeably angular	To smooth out and decrease angles.	Draw a moderate soft arch
	**Square** Width of lower part is the same as the upper	Increase angle, for balance, creating more of a symmetrical look	Enhance the arch with more of a pronounced peak

Before & After

Before, After & Healed

Training

Starting with the proper training is the key to happy clients

Before performing a microblade procedure, it's crucial to have the proper training by a reputable teacher as well as "hands on" experience with models. Being comfortable in the art of microblading is necessary to build a successful business. You'll want your clients to tell their family, friends and co-workers how much they enjoy their natural looking eyebrows that won't wash off.

This manual has been laid out to be part of the educational materials for schools, as well as beginners and advanced microblade artists. A major part of training is gathering relevant information that can be used as an everyday guide.

Shortcuts in life don't work! A new trade takes training and following through with practices. It is necessary to have the proper training that teaches the key elements that should be continually practiced. Mastering the art of drawing simulated hair strokes, and perfecting how to implant color that will obtain excellent healing results is important. Great trainers will emphasis this as well as safety and cleanliness!

Becoming a Successful Microblade Artist through Practice

The goal of the microblade artist is to be able to draw hair strokes that flow with each person's hair pattern. We hear all the time in life, practice if you want to get good at anything. Well, that is exactly what is necessary to succeed in this field.

When it comes to drawing on beautiful eyebrows with simulated hair strokes, working with the flow of each person's hair pattern is important for the design of the eyebrow.

On the following pages you will learn basic eyebrow hair strokes and how to draw popular designs. There are pictures of real eyebrows to practice drawing on.

After you feel you've grasped the art of drawing hair strokes, it's time to practice implanting color on material that simulates skin. There are different products sold by suppliers and are available in a variety of sizes and shapes.

Patience is a virtue when it comes to learning a new trade in life. Take the time to practice and gain self-confidence. You can then reap the rewards!

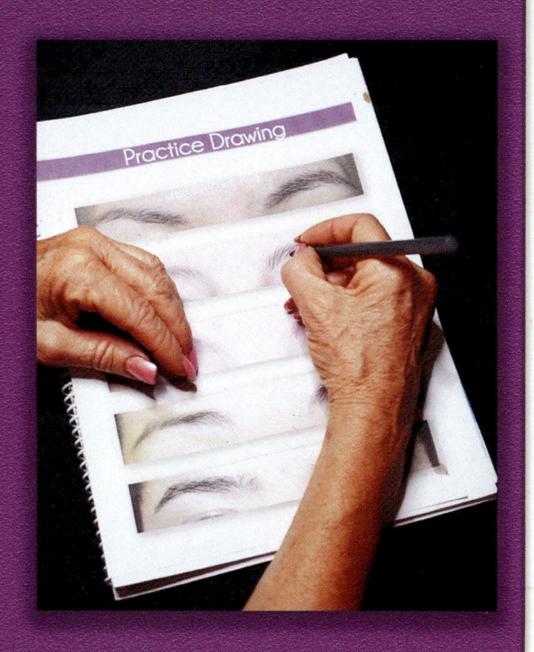

HAIR STROKES

1 - Two Way	2 - Fan Shape

HAIR STROKES

3 - Braided

4 - Uniform

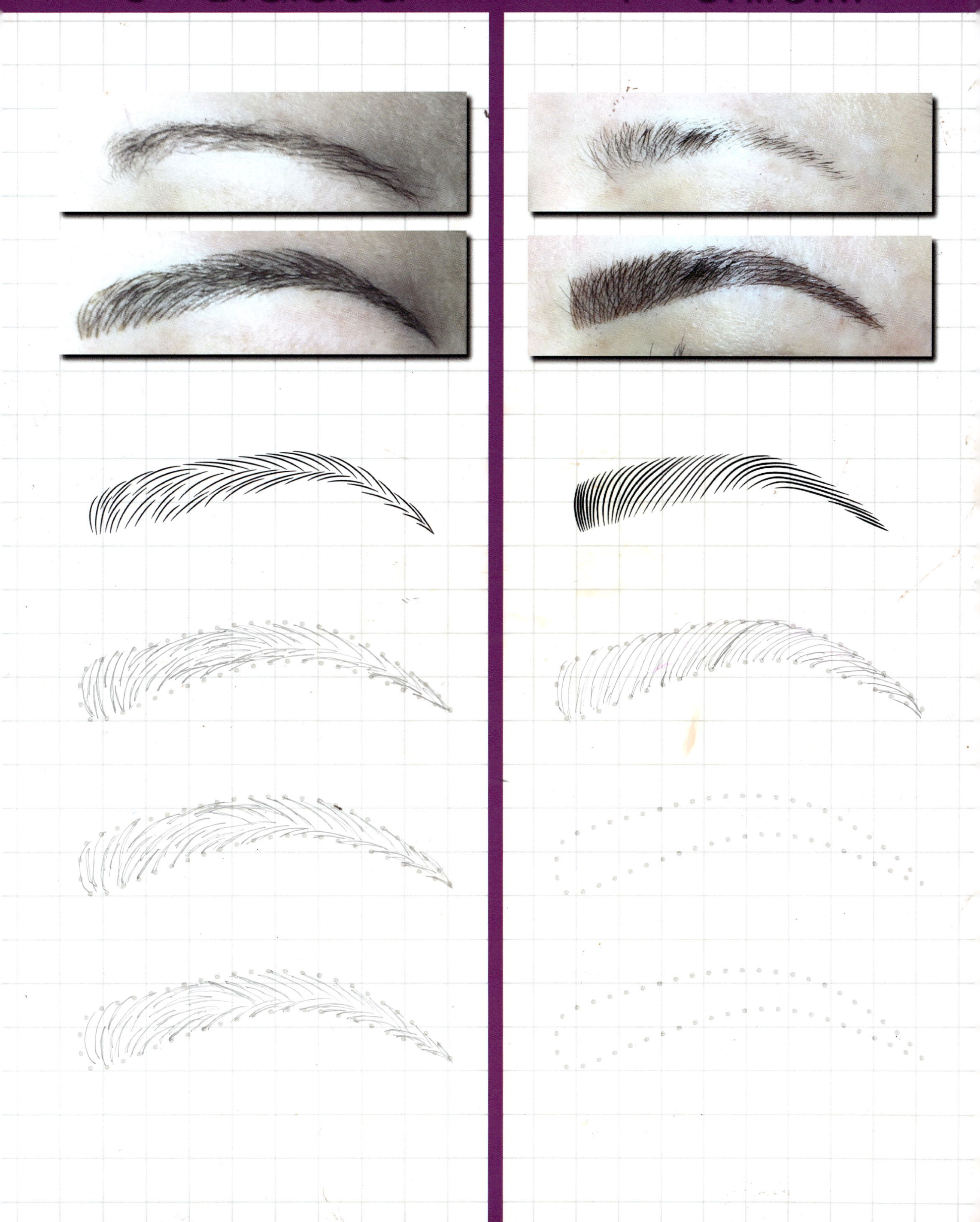

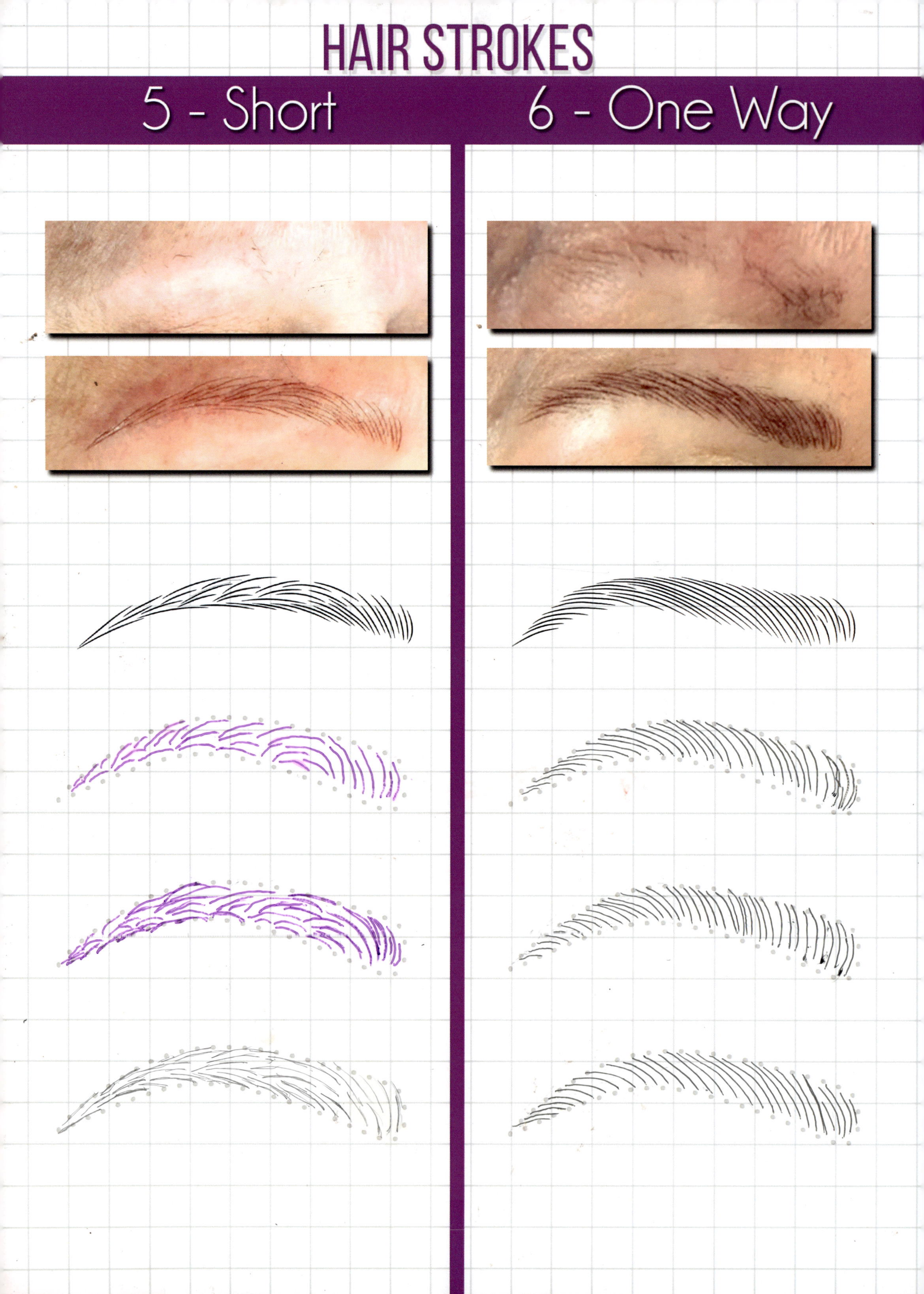
HAIR STROKES
5 - Short
6 - One Way

HAIR STROKES

7 - Shaded | 8 - Full & Shaded

Practice Page

Practice Page

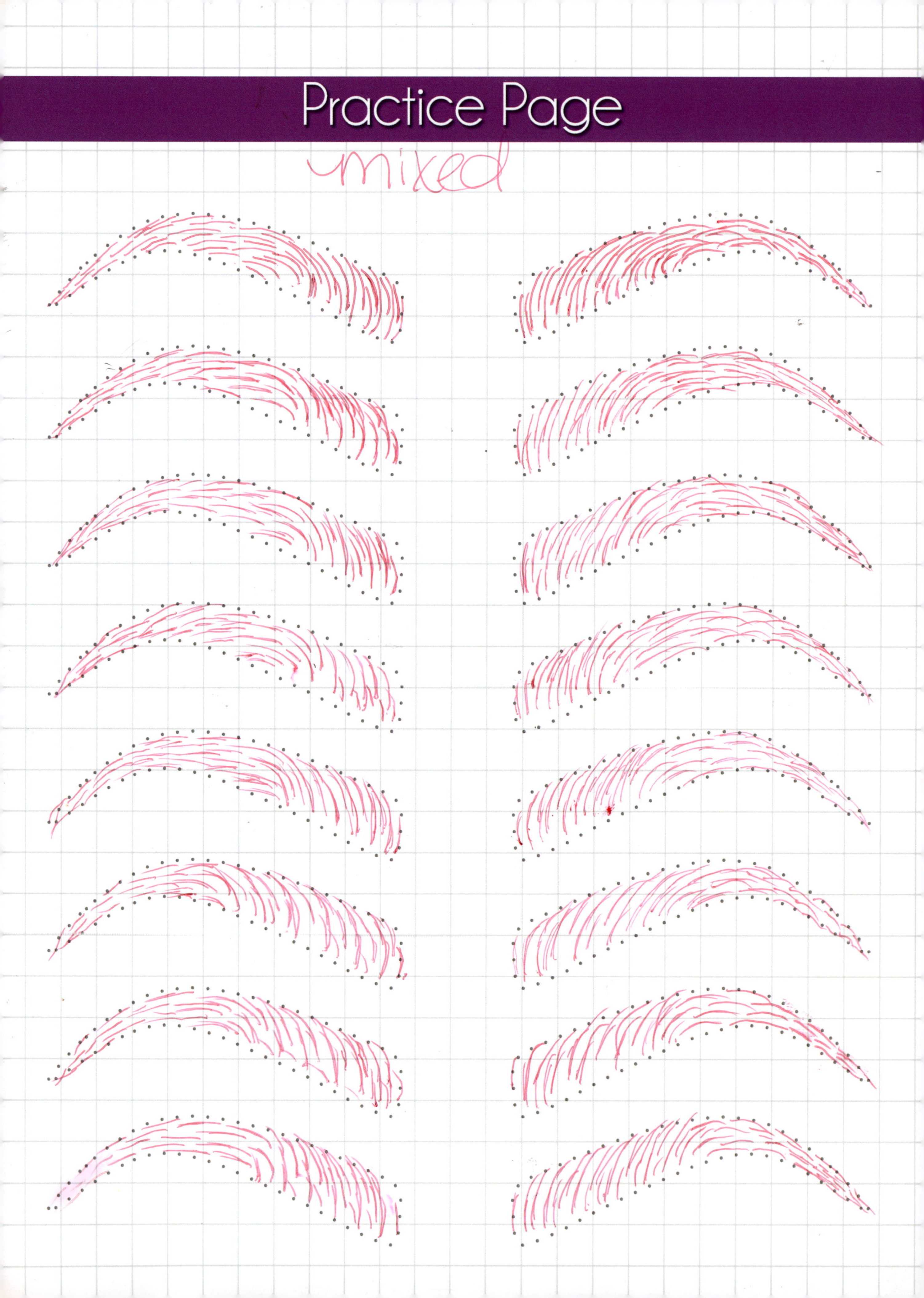
Practice Page
mixed

Practice Page

Uplifting

Practice Drawing

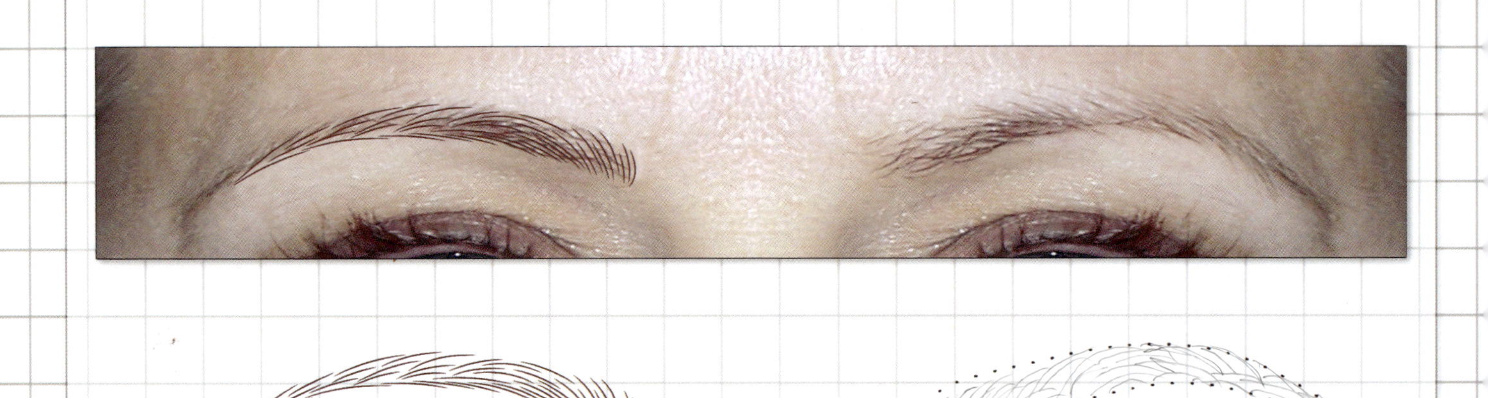

#5 Short Hair Strokes

#4 Uniform Hair Strokes

#2 Fan Shape Hair Strokes

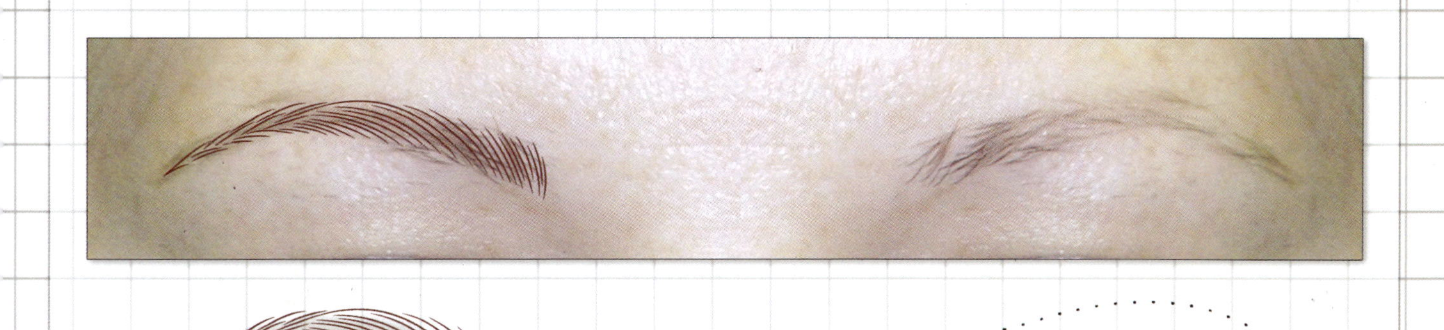

#7 Hair Strokes with Shading

#1 Two Way Hair Strokes

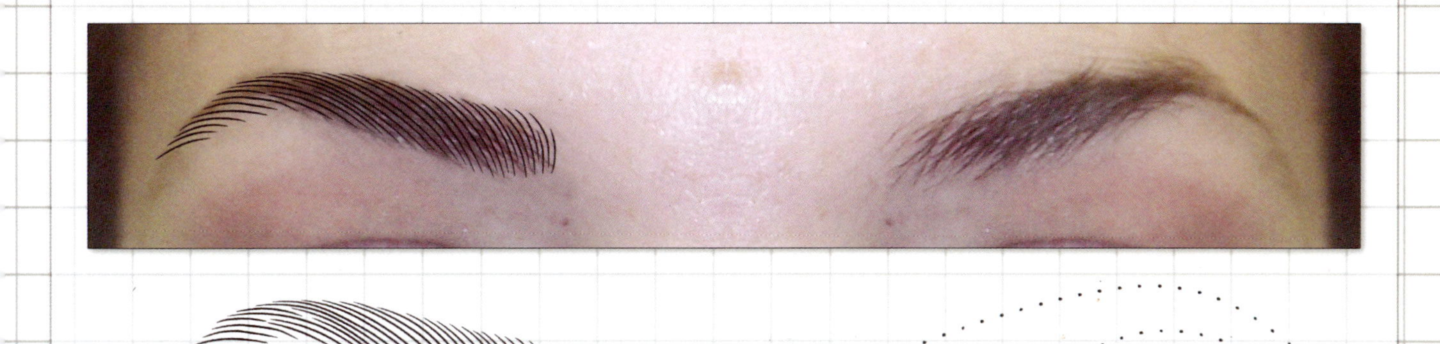

#6 One Way Hair Strokes

Practice Drawing

#4 Uniform Hair Strokes

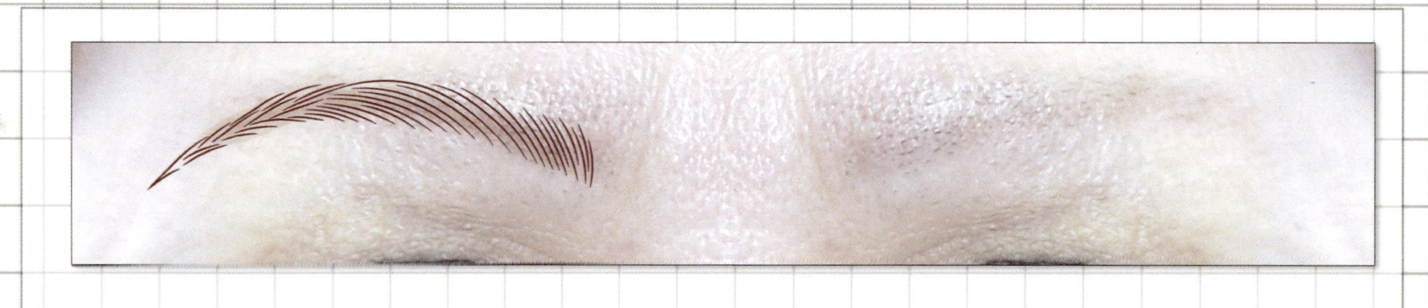

#7 Hair Strokes with Shading

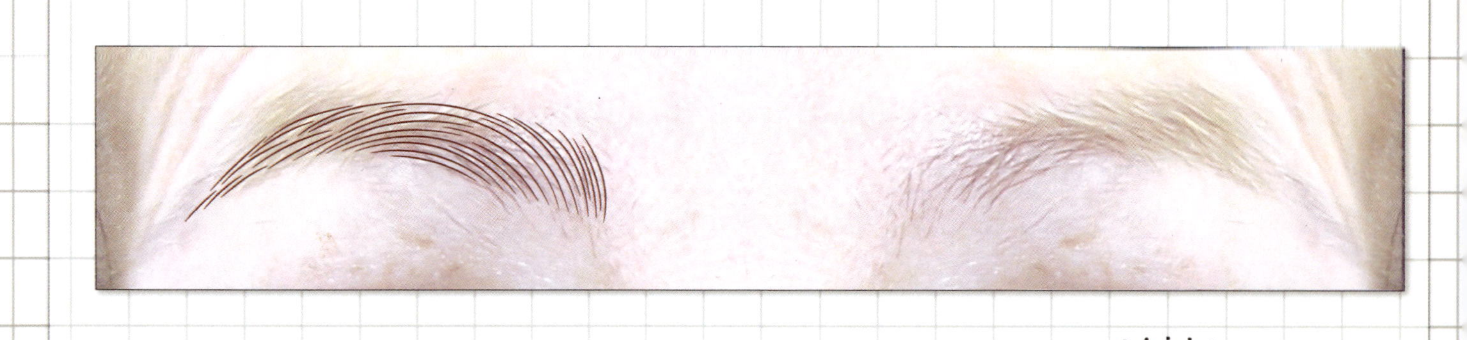

#2 Fan Shape Hair Strokes

Practice Drawing

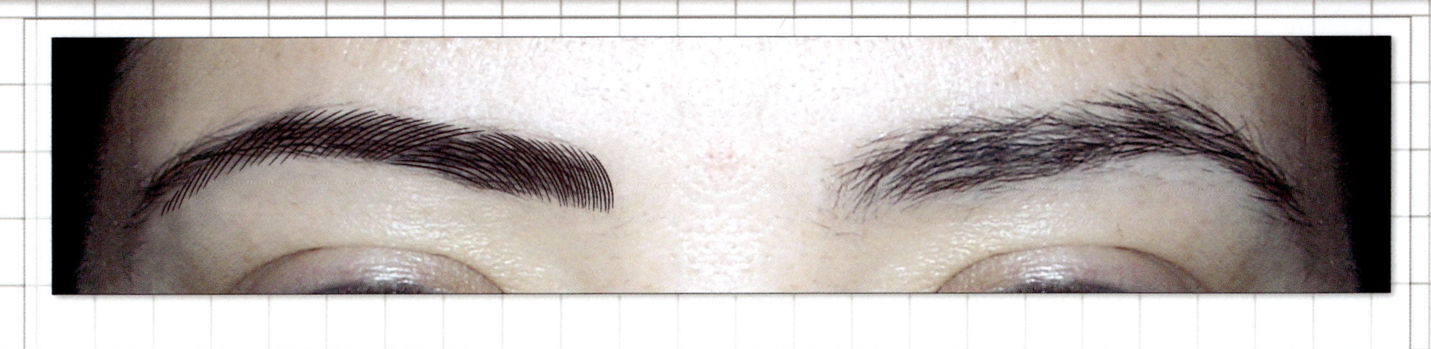

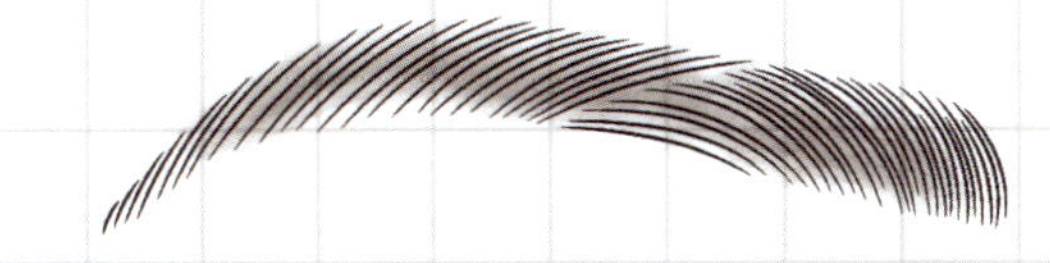

#8 Full Hair Strokes with Shading

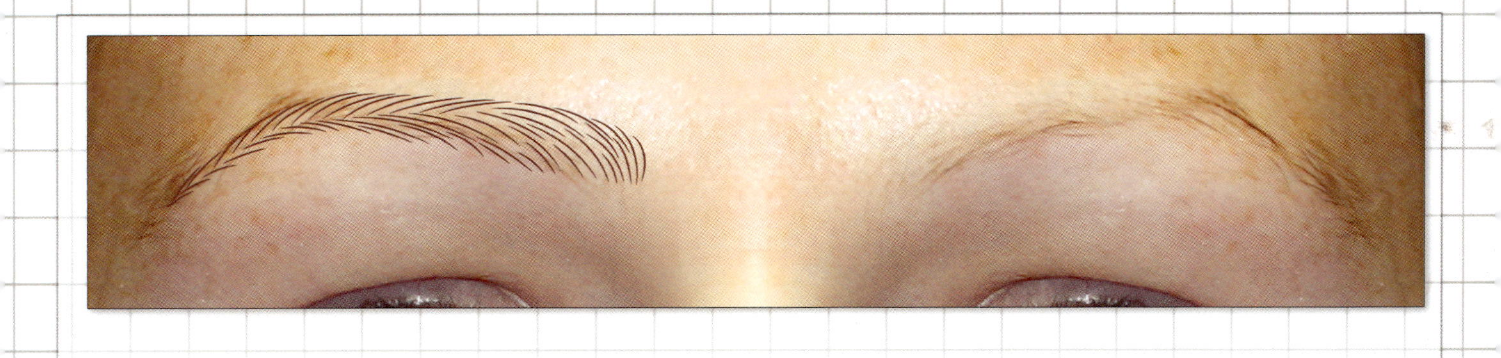

#3 Braided Hair Strokes

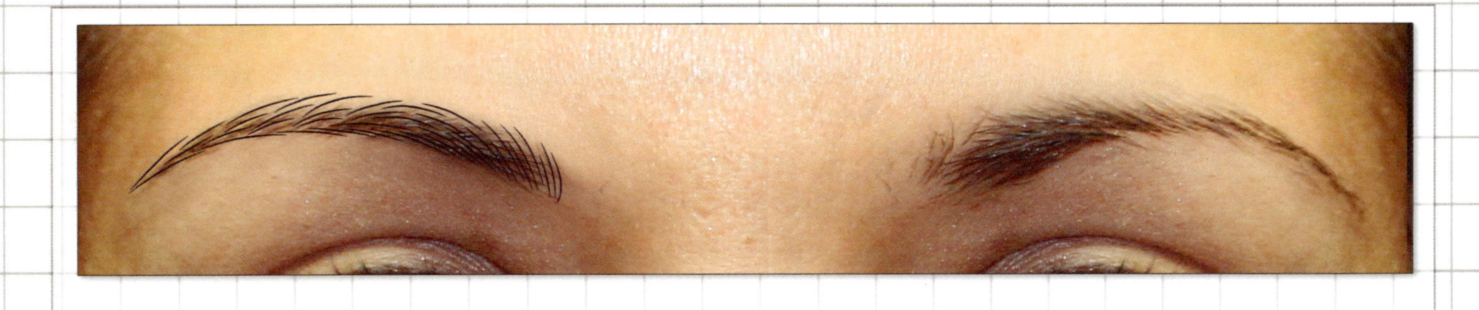

#5 Short Hair Strokes

Practice Drawing

Choose what hair stroke design fits best with each eyebrow hair pattern

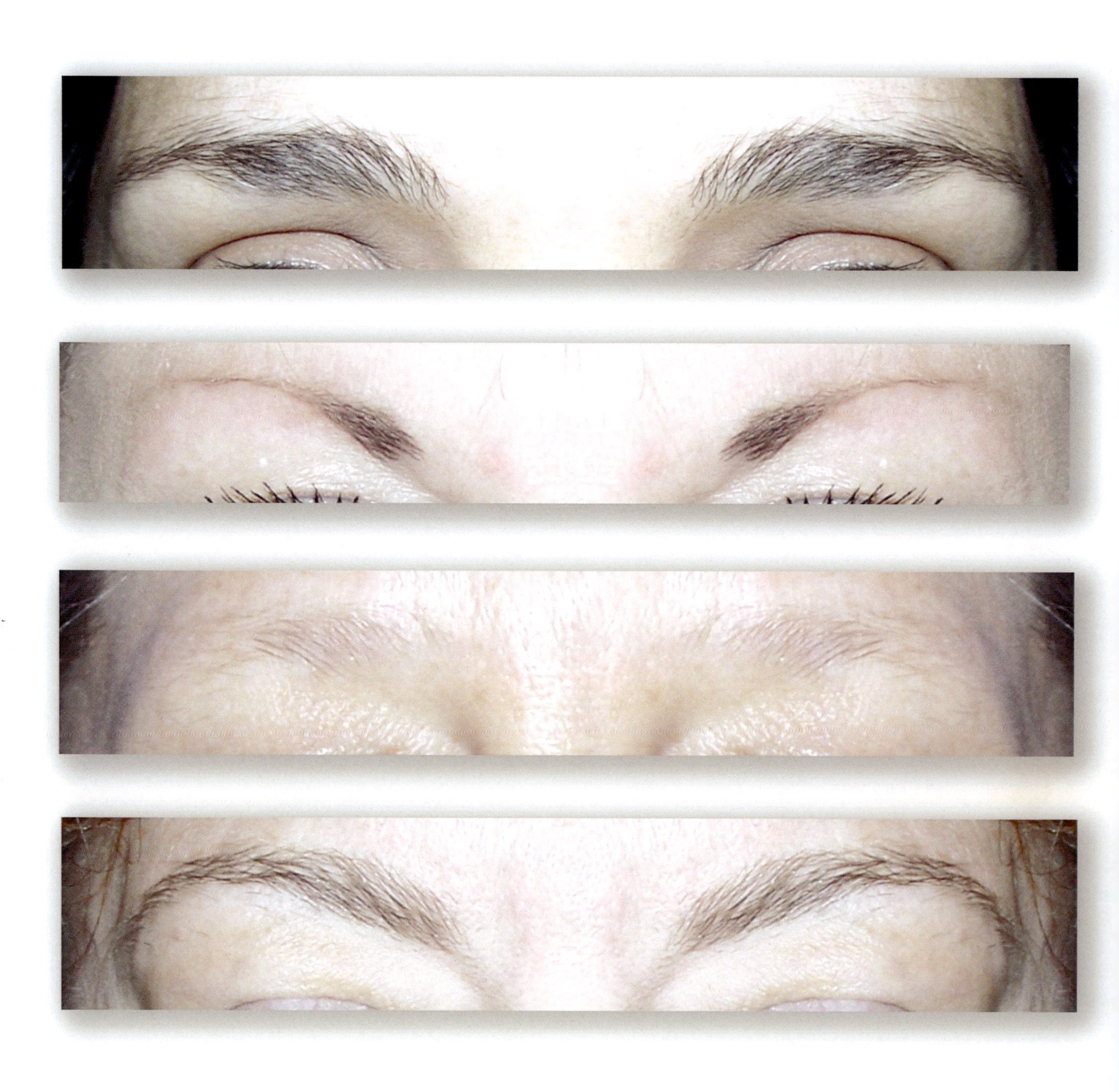

Practice Drawing

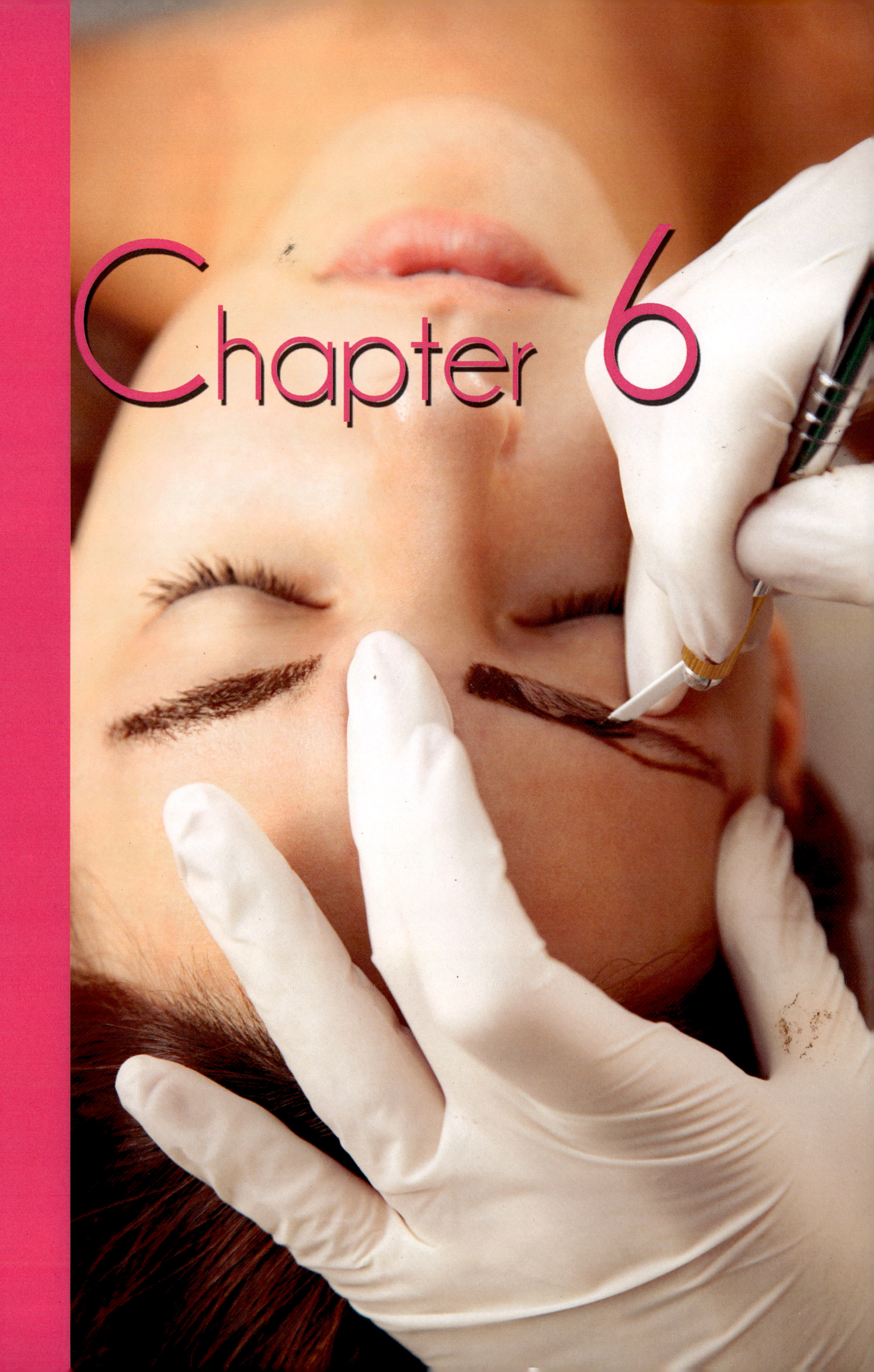

Chapter 6

IMPLANTING COLOR TECHNIQUES

CHAPTER OUTLINE

- Preparation For A Microblade Procedure
- Table Setup And Supplies
- Needles
- Sequence Of A Microblade Procedure For Great Results
- Tips For Implanting Color

IMPLANTING COLOR

A deep aspiration to learn the fundamentals of microblading is needed to advance from a beginner artist to an expert and build a rewarding career. This chapter covers the key techniques necessary to perform a successful microblade procedure. There are many elements you must take into consideration: choosing the right size needles, properly stretching the skin, correct angle, pressure and depth, etc. Perfecting each step of the procedure will help to master the techniques of microblading.

Preparation for a Microblade Procedure

Everything you do for a procedure needs to be synchronized to achieve great results. Clients will brag to their family, friends, and coworkers about their new-found love for their eyebrows, how natural they look and who their professional microblade artist was. The following pages outline the techniques necessary to perform a microblade procedure.

Client and Artist Comfort

In order to perform a procedure both safely and correctly, it's imperative for the artist to be in a comfortable position while working. Equally important, the client needs to be comfortable and in the correct position for the microblade artist to perform and create beautiful eyebrows.

When working on a client, their head should always be leaning back and facing up, chin should not be facing down or their head too far back. This will enable the artist to implant color at the correct angle. No other person in the room should be close enough to interfere, in any way, when a procedure is being performed.

Lighting and Proper Vision Tools

When performing a procedure it's essential to have sufficient overhead lighting correctly positioned above the client's head. It's necessary for the artist to clearly be able to see where to implant each hair stroke. One lighting choice is LED which stays cool to the touch even after use, and can last up to five times longer than most other lights. There should also be sufficient lighting in the room so the artist can see everything, from measuring the eyebrows to the final details.

It's very important to be able to see the spacing of the hair stokes as they are being implanted. Even those who have very good vision may need help seeing details. There are various magnification tools available for an artist who wants to take that extra step to having a clearer view of the area being worked on.

When performing a procedure, it is essential to have sufficient overhead lighting correctly positioned above the client's head.

Table Setup and Supplies

It is important to follow the proper protocols from start to finish:

- Setup for a microblade procedure must include all tools and materials which should be covered or disposed of after each procedure.
- The artist should remove and dispose of gloves each time they leave their work area. Never touch anything during a procedure that can't be disinfected, covered or thrown away after each procedure has been completed.
- After each procedure, the work area should be thoroughly cleaned with a sanitizer. Items which are not thrown away should be wiped down with a disinfectant that kills bacteria and viruses. All needles need to be disposed of in an approved sharps container.

Refer to *Chapter Two Infection Prevention Control Plan* for important information on avoiding the transmission of any possible bloodborne pathogens.

The work area should be clean and setup for each client prior to a procedure. The following is a list of items to have on hand:

Work Area Items

- Work Area Paper or Cloth
- Artist Apron Cover
- Drawing Pencils & Measuring Tools
- Brow Scissors & Tweezers
- Eyebrow Pigments
- Topical Anesthetic
- Pigment Cups and Rings
- Tissues
- Gloves
- Magnifying Glasses
- Moist Wipes & Cotton Swabs
- Microblade Tools
- Disposable Headrest Cover
- Disposable Client Drape
- Plastic Trash Can Liners
- Aftercare Ointment or Cream
- Sharps Waste Container
- Disinfectant
- Barrier Film for Tools

Equipment

- Work Table
- Bed or Recliner
- Chair for Technician
- Headrest for Client
- Overhead Light
- Hand Mirror
- Wall Mirror
- Covered Trash Container

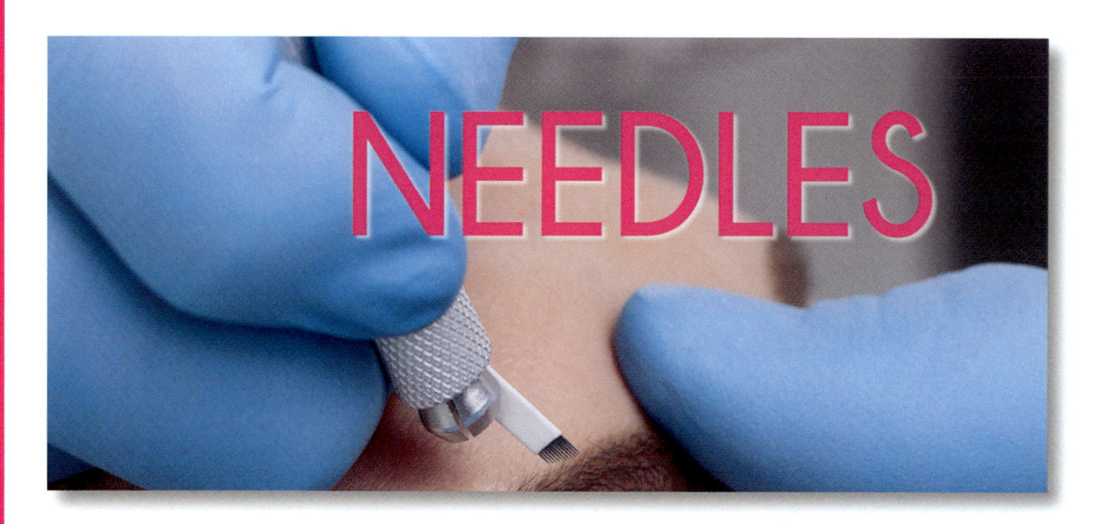

Every microblade artist's goal is to be able to create simulated hair strokes for each client's eyebrows that they will be happy with. First you have to understand what needle combination will be best suited for the different skin types, and hair patterns you could encounter.

Needle Quality and Sterilization

There are many types and styles of needles that artists can purchase. It is important to make sure they're coming from a reputable supplier to ensure the quality and safety of each needle. Pay close attention to damaged or defective needles which may have split or separated. Damaged needles can cause extra bleeding, scar tissue and/or skin damage. Before beginning a procedure, use a small magnifying glass or eye loupe to view each configuration of needles to be sure they are in good condition. This will help avoid any unnecessary trauma to the skin.

Health departments require all microblade tools to be properly disposed of in a sharps waste container after each procedure. The only exception would be if the handle was sterilized in an autoclave.

Choices of Microblade Tools

Through experience, artists will find which combination of needles and tools work best for them. When selecting needles, it is important to consider skin type and how you want your hair strokes to look. Hand tools are available in different styles and shapes as well as the number of needles per tool. The needles and handles that hold them can also be purchased separately. This selection gives an artist a nice variety of choices to create the perfect hair strokes for each client's needs.

Needle size

There are a varity of needles available that create different shapes and sizes of hair strokes. The size of a needle is determined by the number of needles in the configuration and the gauge of the each needle. The difference between smaller and larger needles are:

Smaller Needles offer better color absorption. The needles slice into the skin easily, but there is a chance of slicing the skin too deep.

Larger Needles create a thicker looking hair stroke which makes them appear more intense and bolder.

Slant

Strength of Needles

The thickness of a client's skin will determine the needle strength needed. There are two to choose from:

Slope

Flexible Needles are popular. They cater to thinner mature skin. Because of their flexibility, they are also used for practicing.

Hard Needles are for bolder hair strokes. With hard needles, strokes tend to penetrate easily into the skin; so minimum pressure is needed. A hard needle is usually used for darker, thicker, and/or oily skin.

Needle Configurations

The microblade artist has a choice of what needles to use for hair strokes, any detailed work needed and shading, if requested. Here are few popular needle configurations:

U Shape

Slant Needles are a practical design that can be used on most people. It's a popular needle configuration. It can be used to get those crisp lines along the bottom of the eyebrows.

Slope Needles have a curved angle for a precision root stroke design, allowing a curved stroking motion. The tip of the needles make a smooth entry point to create lines that make fine hair strokes.

U Shape Needles are designed for more detailed hair strokes. They are usually used toward the end of the procedure to create wispy hair strokes. It's a favorite with the more experienced artist. The rounded edge helps make a curved stroke, and since the angle of the needles has no starting and stopping points, it gives a soft, rounded finish.

Shader

Shader Needles are used to add more of a shaded effect between the hair strokes. It is called shader needles because it finishes the eyebrows with a more filled-in look and adds depth as well. The shader needles come in different shapes and needle counts. The design consists of needles placed together in a round staggered configuration, flat and with two rows of needles.

Sequence of a Microblade Procedure

There is an art to performing a microblade procedure, from drawing the eyebrows and knowing what color is best for each client, to executing the steps for the procedure itself. It's necessary to master the correct techniques for achieving beautiful, natural looking eyebrows that will satisfy each client.

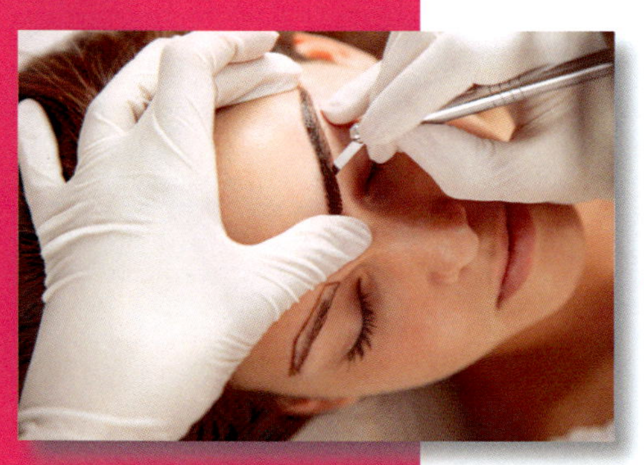

Stretching

Everything that has just been read up to this point has helped prepare for the moment of actually implanting beautiful, simulated hair strokes. The following is the sequence of importance:

Stretching the Skin

Before beginning to implant color, be sure the skin is stretched properly. This will help ensure smooth and evenly healed hair strokes. One of the ways to stretch the skin is as follows:

- Use the hand not holding the tool, and with your thumb and middle or index finger, stretch the skin above the eyebrow. Flatten skin with a taut stretch.
- With the working hand, use your pinky to stretch the skin downward.

This will give a perfect three-way stretch, enabling you to have a firm area in which to implant crisp, fine hair strokes. Keep this same stretch throughout the procedure. Stretching the skin in this way will help strokes to be smooth and not bounce. Also, it will keep the hair strokes from looking blurred when healed.

Placement and Angle of the Microblade Tool

When implanting color, it's important to have the proper angle and placement of the microblade tool. The following is the correct way to hold and angle a microblade tool:

- A microblade tool should be held like a pen at a 90 degree angle as seen in the picture on the following page.
- The handle should be in an upright position, not leaning to the left or right. If the needles lean in either direction, it will cause the hair stroke color to heal blurred.
- Each needle placement must make the same full contact on flat, stretched skin at all times.

Use Consistent Pressure

With the microblading tool, always apply consistent pressure. Uneven color will occur if any of the needles are not equally touching the skin. When using sharp, quality needles, and very little pressure, you should be able to glide the needles softly through the skin to form each hair stroke.

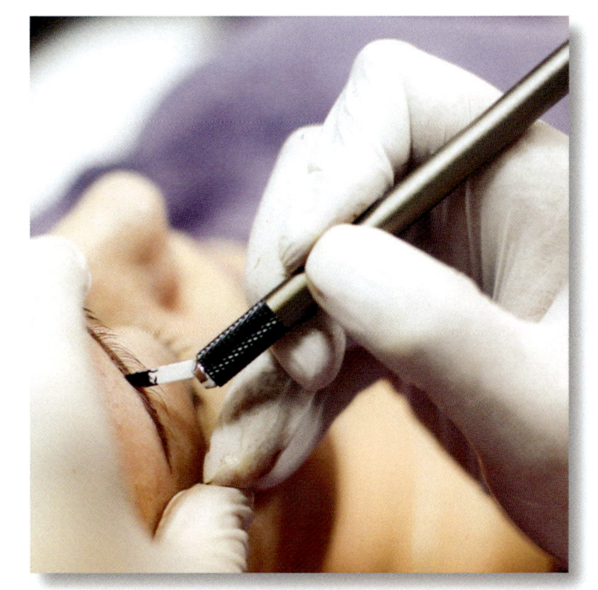

90° Angle

The thickness of a person's skin may make it necessary to adjust the pressure. The skin in the front part of the eyebrow, known as the crown, can be a little thicker. Therefore, it may be necessary to slightly increase pressure. However, less pressure is needed when using a smaller configuration of needles. Here are three basic skin types with the pressure that is best to use:

Thin - The age and the ethnicity of a client may cause the skin to be thinner, therefore a lighter pressure is required.

Normal - Normal thickness will require a gentle, even, medium pressure throughout each stroke.

Thick - Oily and darker skin can cause skin to be a little thicker, so it may be necessary to apply slightly more pressure. It will also depend on which needles have been chosen to do the procedure as well.

Some people naturally bleed more than others. However, if the area where color is being implanted needs constant wiping because of bleeding, it may be because too much pressure is being used. This can cause the needles to reach the deeper dermis layer of the skin where the blood vessels are. If there is too much pressure being used, the following may occur:

- Heavy bleeding
- Hair strokes look blurred after they heal
- Color "blow out" (where color can spread outside of the intended area)
- Skin may form scar tissue
- Hair strokes heal an unnatural grayish color

Pace in Which to Implant Color

Keeping a slow and consistent pace while performing a procedure is crucial. If the color is implanted too quickly, it will not grab. This is where deep concentration comes into play. Learning to control and execute the correct speed needed for implanting color for each hair stroke is important for a successful outcome.

Depth in Which to Implant Color

The depth of each stroke is determined by the microblade artist. Understanding the skin layers and being able to find the correct "Sweet Spot" or "Target Zone," takes dedication and practice. Refer to *Chapter Two Skin Anatomy* to read more about the structure and the papillary dermis layer of skin, where the color needs to be implanted.

A good gauge for checking the depth of a stroke, is to slightly spread it apart after it has been passed through and soaked with color. If the split opens evenly and has color in it with very minimal bleeding, the color has been placed properly. The big question most artists have is how to determine if enough color has been implanted into the papillary dermis layer of the skin. Because the "Art of Microblading" is just that, an art, there is really no way to determine the right amount of color. It takes a lot of practice and paying close attention to your client's healed results. It is important to never over work the skin, the less trauma to the skin the better the results.

Implanting the Color and Needle Usage

The key is to be prepared before performing your first and every microblade procedure thereafter. Let's take a look again at the important techniques of a procedure:

Stretching - Stretch the skin in three different directions for firmness.

Placement and Angle - The microblade tool needs to be held like a pen, at a 90 degree angle, making full contact with the skin.

Using Consistent Pressure - Use the same consistent pressure, only adjusting for skin type if needed.

Working Pace - Keep a slow and consistent pace throughout the procedure.

Depth of Implanting Color - Keep the depth of each stroke consistent; the pressure used will determine the depth of the color being implanted. The goal is the upper dermis layer of the skin.

After your client has been properly numbed, start the procedure. Here is a suggested guideline for implanting color:

Dip for Color - Dip the needles into a finger ring or a pigment cup of color.

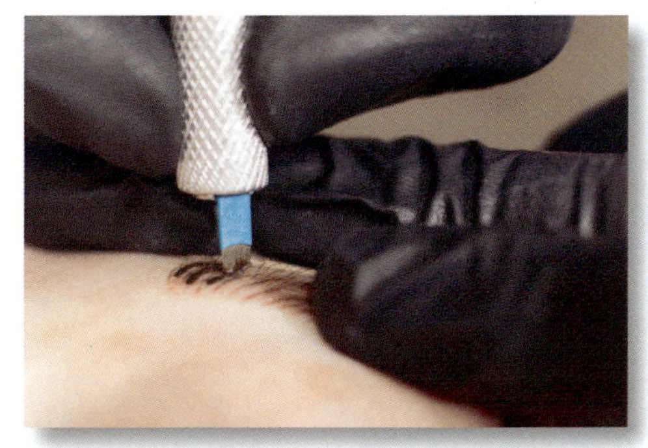

Gently Glide the Needles - Begin at the root part of the hair stroke and start your first stroke. With the three point stretch in place and the microblade needles making full, even contact with the skin, gently glide the needles pulling through each stroke with smooth, even pressure. Let the needles do the work. Finish each stroke with a sweeping motion, lifting the needles off the skin to finish the hair stroke.

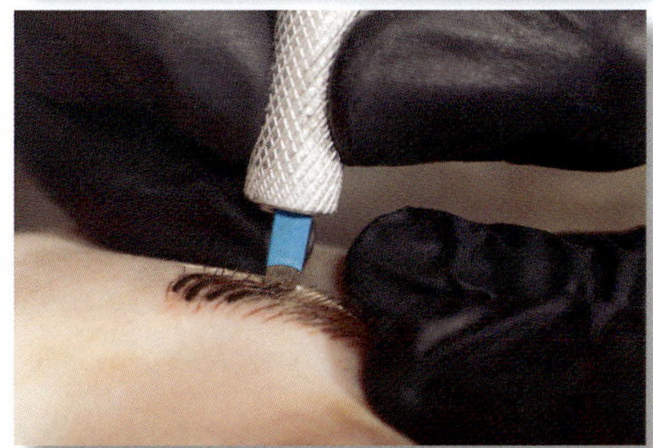

First Pass of Color - Implant the first pass of hair strokes until there is enough color for a guide. If you are not using a skin-safe marker to ourline the eyebrow shape, this will help ensure you have a guide as you're drawing wipes off.

Soak with Color - Use a clean cotton swab or applicator to apply more color over the open hair strokes a couple times during and at the end of the procedure. Leave on the skin for 3-5 minutes, allowing the skin to absorb the color. With a wipe, clean off excess color from the eyebrow and the surrounding skin.

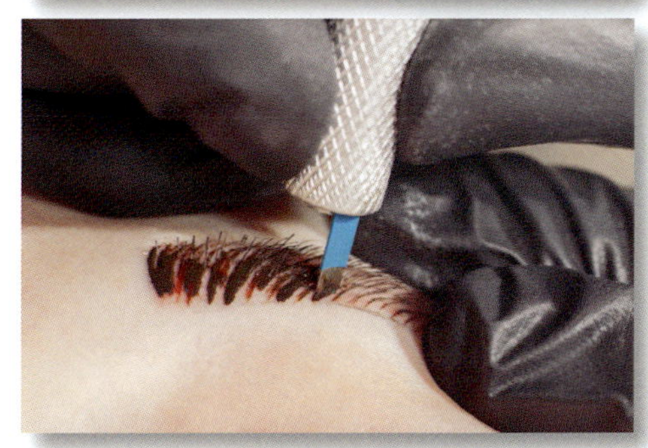

Check Needles - Throughout the procedure, check needles, and wipe them to be sure they are clean and free of excess color build up and skin particles.

Continue Implanting Color - For a sparse look, keep extra space between each hair stroke. For a fuller look, place the strokes closer together. Continue to implant hair strokes until you have the look you want to achieve. Finish with detailed hair strokes, add shading if requested.

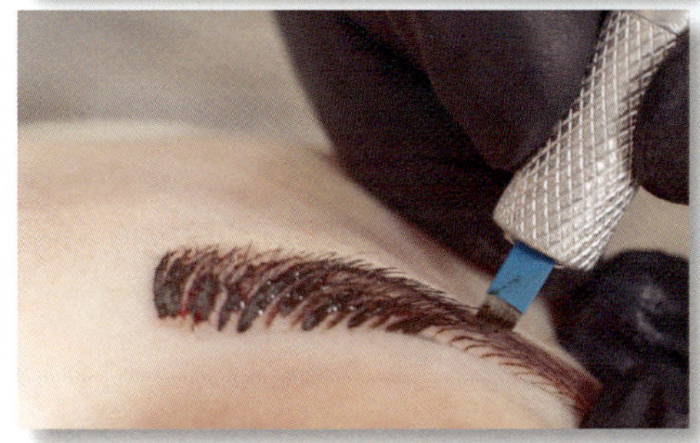

By simultaneously applying all the key points, along with dedication to practicing, each client will be able to show off their beautiful, natural looking eyebrows. For an overall view on the steps for a microblade procedure, refer to *Chapter Seven Steps for an Microblade Procedure.*

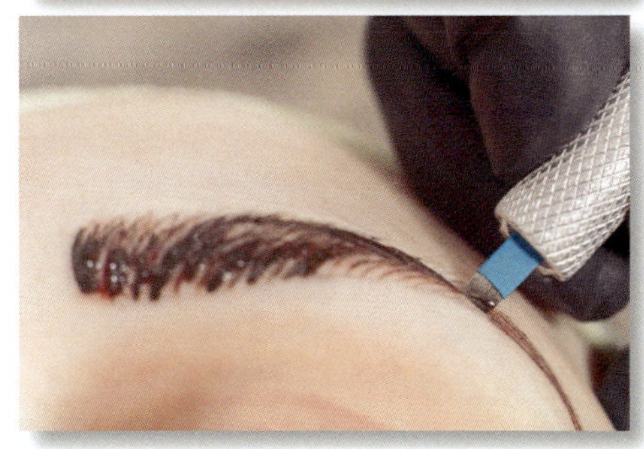

Implanting Color for a 3D effect

To give the dimension of a 3D effect, use your creativity to add sparse hair strokes throughout the eyebrows with lighter or darker colors. This can be done with needles that have their own style like U-shaped needles for a finishing effect.

Shading Technique

To fill in the eyebrows with soft color in between the hair strokes, use a shader tool, as seen in the needle section on page 90 and 91. When using a round staggered needle configuration it gives a stippling effect by adding small dots of color that blend together to shade in an area. This adds more color, creating a filled in, powdery look to the eyebrows.

To apply the shading effect with these needles use a soft tapping motion, keeping the color toward the middle of the eyebrows. This will allow the needles to deposit dots of color between the strokes, leaving a nice shadow of color when the area heals. By using a wetting solution, sold by microblade supply companies, color can be diluted up to 25-50% to give a more subtle result. Be sure to never over work the eyebrow area, or use too much pressure when you are implanting color for a shading effect, as it may take away from the design of the eyebrow itself. There are other shading tools such as flat and double row needle configurations.

Wipe and Clean as You Go

Because of the excess color and any light bleeding that could occur while performing a microblade procedure, it's necessary to continually wipe the area where you are applying color. You need to clearly see where each hair stroke is being implanted, and the distance between each one. This is important for the eyebrows to look natural.

It's crucial to maintain a clean work area at all times. Never place anything that's been used back on the work area. If using wipes, cut into small pieces, throw each piece away after use. This pertains to your needles as well. Be sure the needles are clean of any dried pigment or skin particles. Wipe the needles throughout the procedure, as clean needles will make clean hair strokes. This is not only for sanitary purposes, but clean tools and a clean work area make it easier to perform procedures and allows you to be creative.

7 TIPS TO REMEMBER WHEN IMPLANTING COLOR

1. The main mistake artists can make when performing a microblade procedure, is using too much pressure. There should be a very minimal amount of bleeding. Trauma to the skin from needles could cause scarring.

2. When implanting color for a powdery effect, avoid placing color too close to the edge of the eyebrow. Also, do not use too much pressure, as it will cause color to heal darker than the hair strokes implanted.

3. For thin to average skin, use smaller needle configurations for finer hair strokes. For thicker more dramatic hair strokes, use larger needle configurations.

4. When implanting color, keep the microblade tool at a 90 degree angle. Hair strokes will heal blurred if they are implanted with the tool leaning to one side or another.

5. To properly implant crisp, fine hair strokes, it's important to use a firm three point stretch.

6. Try to avoid crisscrossing hair strokes because it could cause the color to heal blurred.

7. It's important to soak the skin with color at least twice during the procedure, and once at the end for 3 to 5 minutes.

Chapter 7

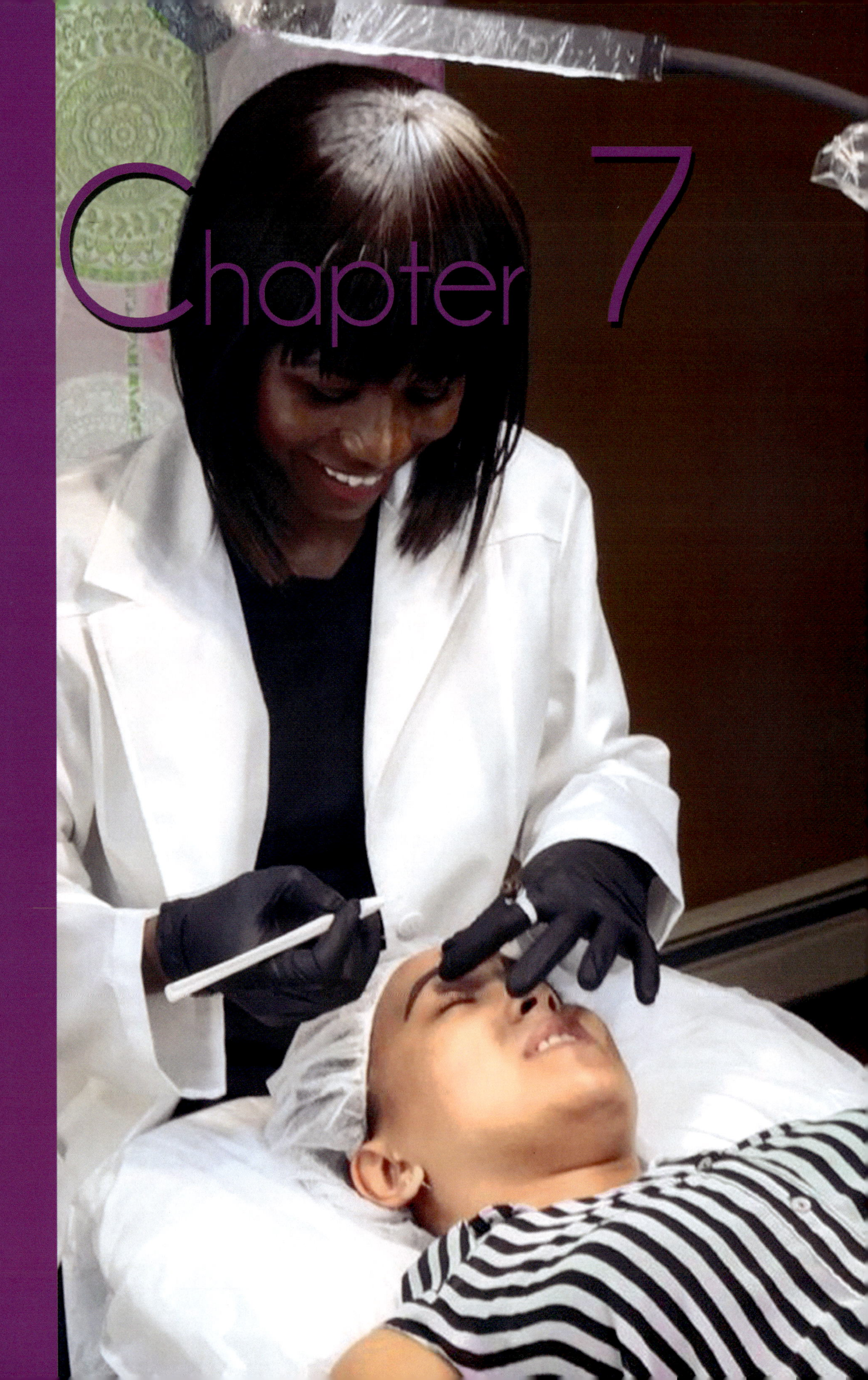

STEPS FOR A MICROBLADE PROCEDURE

CHAPTER OUTLINE

- Getting Ready For An Eyebrow Procedure
- Steps For An Eyebrow Procedure
- Eyebrow Outline For A Procedure
- Implanting Color

STEPS FOR AN EYEBROW PROCEDURE

Before you start a procedure, there are a few things that need to be accomplished:

- Make sure the work station has been sterilized and prepared for a microblade procedure.
- Have clients fill out the necessary paperwork and answer any questions they may have.
- Take a "before" picture.
- Review client's expectations.
- Clean the client's eyebrows.

There are ten steps to performing a microblade procedure. They are as follows:

Step 1 - Draw and Measure

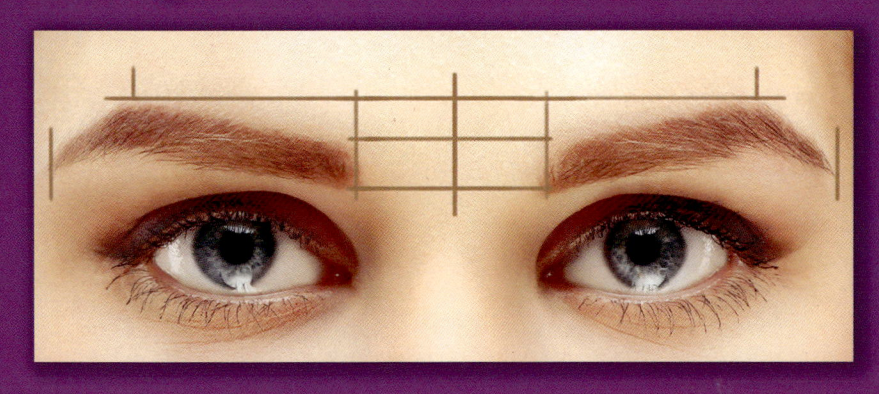

Do a visual measuring first, then draw on the eyebrows for your client to see. After receiving the approval, measure the eyebrows and draw guidelines. Here are a few different ways an artist can prepare the eyebrows for the client's approval:

- Draw on and fill in the eyebrows. This shows the client the shape and how they will look with color (showcasing where the hair strokes will be placed), as seen in the picture
- Following the outside shape of the eyebrows that were drawn on, draw a guideline around where the hair strokes will be placed.

If necessary, and with the client's permission, tweeze the eyebrows where needed. This will help you see the shape of the eyebrows. Stand in front of a wall mirror with your client to view the eyebrows. After the client has given their approved, it is important to measure the eyebrows to ensure they are even. Refer to *Chapter Five Drawing Hair Strokes* for measuring tools, tips and a hands-on practice section.

Step 2 - Draw an Outlines

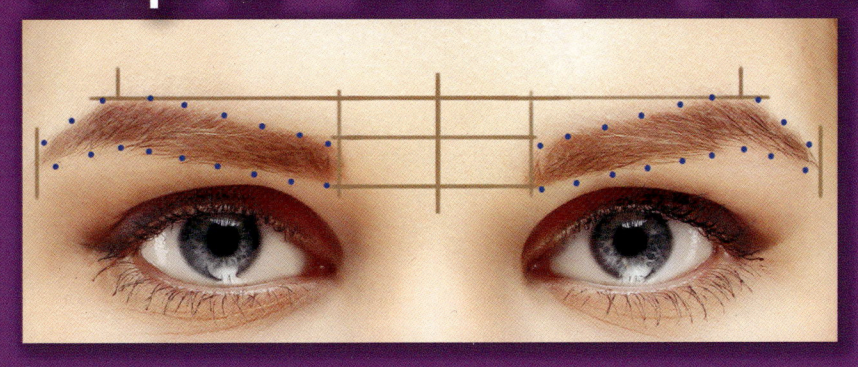

Once you start implanting the color, you do not want to compromise the beautiful eyebrows you have perfectly shaped. Outline each eyebrow with a skin-safe marker that won't easily wash off during a procedure. As the measuring pencil lines wipe off, the marker outline will remain. This will help ensure the color is implanted evenly in the intended area. Surgical markers work well because they don't easily wipe off. There are special erasers available to remove any remaining marks. Here are a couple of ways to outline the eyebrows after measuring them:

- With a marker, outline the eyebrows by placing dots around the exact shape of how they have been drawn on, as shown in the picture.
- Use a marker to draw a solid line to outline the shape where the hair strokes will be implanted.

Step 3 - Apply Topical Anesthetic "Prior" to a Procedure

Using a cotton swab, apply the topical anesthetic "prior" to a procedure on both eyebrows. When applying topical anesthetic, avoid touching the outline that was drawn on with a marker to prevent causing the outline to dissolve. This is a good time to review, confirm the procedure with the client and prepare the eyebrow color(s).

Step 4 - Implant the Color

- Before implanting color, use a magnifying glass or eye loupe to double check that needles are not defective.
- When implanting color, it's essential to use the correct three-point stretching technique, while firmly holding the skin.
- A microblade tool needs to be held at a 90 degree angle to ensure the hair strokes are implanted correctly.
- Start with light, consistent pressure, slowly gliding the needles through each hair stroke.

Refer to *Chapter Six Implanting Color Techniques* for important tips, and needle usage.

Step 5 - Soak with Color

A couple times during a procedure and once at the end, apply color over the hair strokes you have implanted. Let color soak for 3 to 5 minutes. After that, the skin begins to close and the color won't soak in. Wipe the area clean to reveal beautiful hair strokes.

Step 6 - Focus on Technique

It is important to recheck the implanting techniques during the procedure for ultimate results. Here are a few to focus on.

- Keep skin firmly stretched to enable the needles to penetrate and not bounce.
- Check placement of the tool, making sure it is not leaning to either side. This will help avoid colors healing with a blurred look.
- Use light pressure. There should be very minimal bleeding, if any.
- Keep a slow pace to help ensure color grabbing.

Step 7 - Apply Topical Anesthetic

It's important to help keep your client as comfortable as possible "during" the procedure. Keep an open line of communication. Let your client know you can re-apply the topical anesthetic if they are uncomfortable.

Step 8 - Check for Even Eyebrows

Have the client sit up a few times during the procedure to check to make sure both eyebrows are even. Eyebrows look different on a person when they are lying down, versus sitting up and seeing them straight on. It's important to be able to see the eyebrows and get an overall picture of the design you want to accomplish. Make any adjustments, adding more hair strokes as needed.

Step 9 - Finish Implanting Color

On the final passes, add any details necessary to complete the shape. If the client requests a more powdery (or filled-in) look, use a shading tool, avoiding the outside edges. To prevent the shading effect healing darker than hair strokes, be sure to maintain consistent, light pressure. Refer to page 91 for the selection of shading needle configuration and page 96 for shading technique.

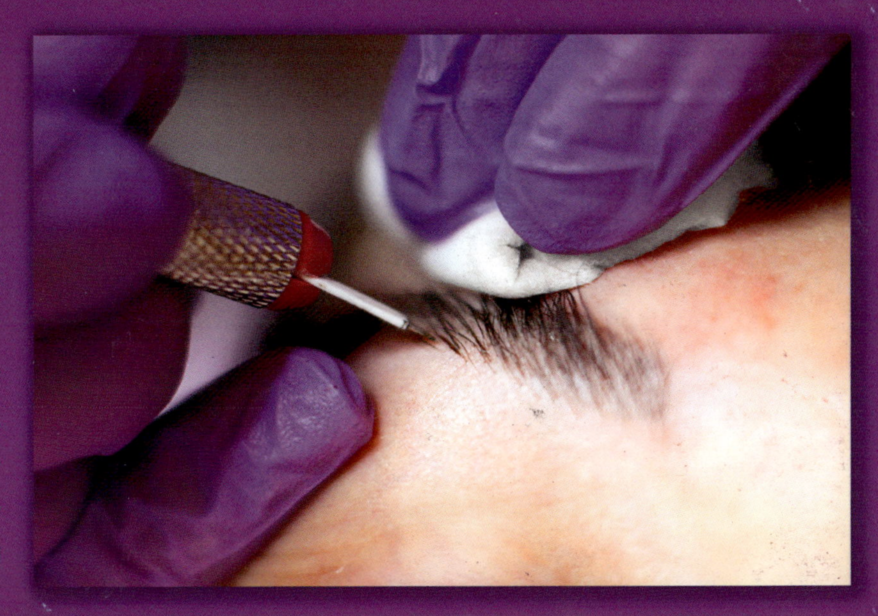

Step 10 - Show Your Client Their Beautiful New Eyebrows

Here are a few steps to take when the eyebrow procedure is finished:

- It's good practice for both you and your client to stand in front of a wall mirror again, to get approval and admire their new eyebrows. Your client will be a walking advertisement, showing off their beautiful eyebrows and letting people know who their microblade artist was.
- Once the client has given their approval, do the final color soaking.
- Go over aftercare instructions.
- Take their "after" picture.
- Apply the aftercare ointment.
- Reassure your client that their color will lighten, and look softer when it heals in approximately a week.
- Follow the proper protocol to clean your work area and dispose of all necessary items to avoid chance of any contamination.

Refer to Chapter Two Infection Prevention Control Plan for more information on a sterilized work station.

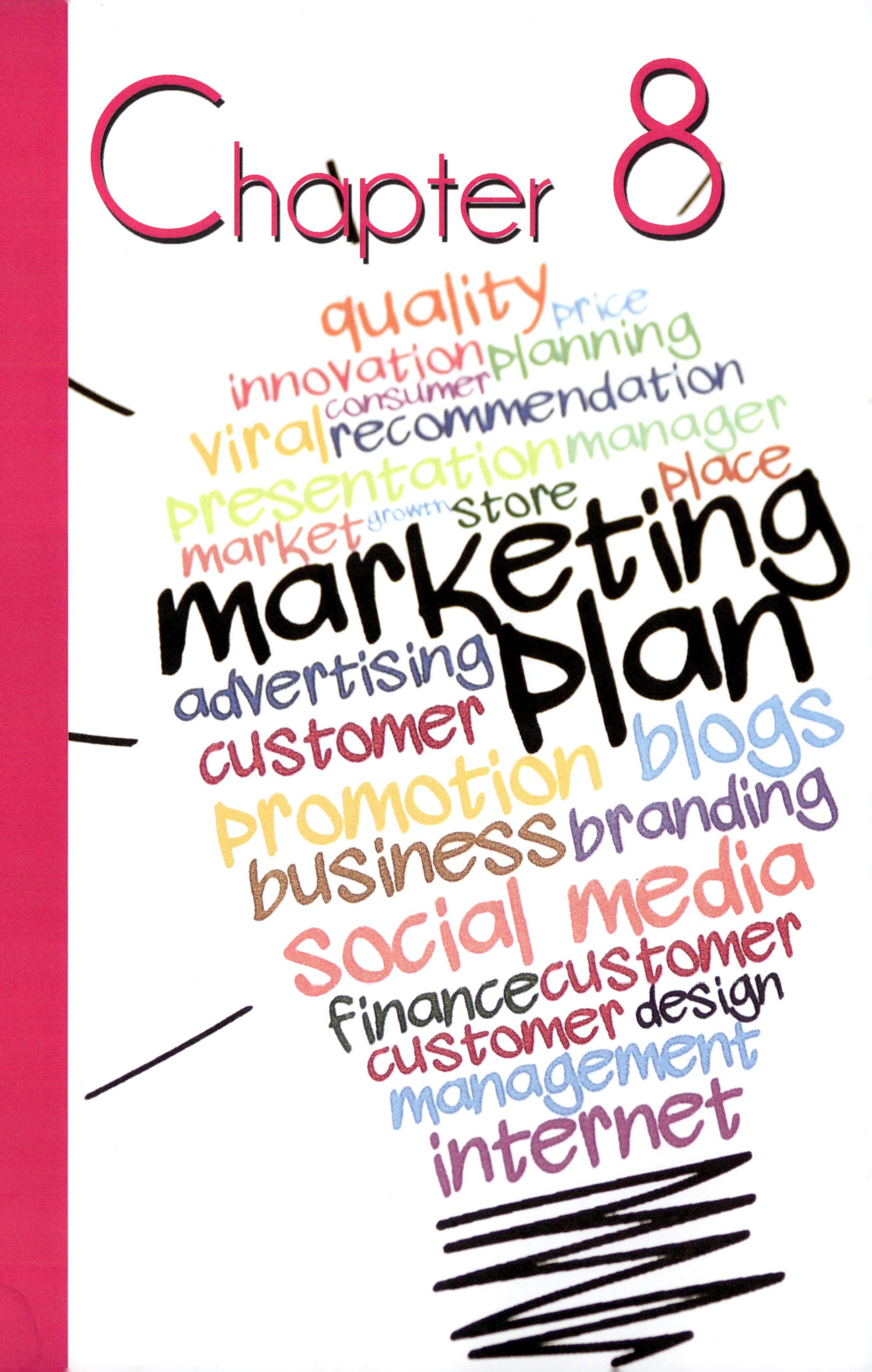
Chapter 8
quality
price
innovation
planning
consumer
viral
recommendation
presentation
manager
place
market
growth
store
marketing
plan
advertising
customer
blogs
promotion
business
branding
social media
finance
customer
customer
design
management
internet

MARKETING YOUR BUSINESS

CHAPTER OUTLINE

- Marketing Strategy
- Online Marketing
- Search Engine Optimization
- The Importance Of A Website
- Clients Are Walking Advertisements

MARKETING YOUR BUSINESS

When you are trying to market a microblading business it's important to sell your service as well as the quality of work you do. This can be done on the internet and various other marketing avenues. Being prepared with the right marketing material is always the first thing that needs to be accomplished. As stated earlier in chapter one, the importance of choosing the correct pictures for marketing purposes is essential. Always think about what your consumers are going to want to view on your website and marketing material. Think about what you would want to see when you are looking for a new service such as pictures, testimonials, reviews, professional look etc. In today's world, people move fast, they think quickly and they even make up their mind that they dislike something even faster. Having a clean but informative and eye catching website is the key. In this chapter we will go over different methods to market a business and the importance of various platforms on the internet.

Marketing Strategy

Marketing strategy includes the basic and long-term activities in the field of marketing that will contribute to your business goals. The focus of your strategy should be making sure that your services meet your clients' needs and developing long-term and profitable relationships with those clients. The next step is to draw up a detailed marketing plan that sets out the specific actions to put that strategy into practice. Questions to ask when developing your strategy:

- What do I want to achieve? Set clear and realistic objectives.
- How will I target the right potential customers?
- How can I improve my customer service?
- What should my price be so I am competitive?
- Should I have seasonal specials?
- What are ways for target audiences to find out about my services?
- Should I include other products or services to increase sales and profitability?
- How can I tell if my marketing is effective?

The following page is a calendar with some of the marketing ideas you will find in this chapter showing you an example of how to put a marketing plan into action.

MARKETING

SUN	MON	TUE	WED	THU	FRI	SAT
26	27	28	29	30	31	1
Look over business plan add to calendar 2	Follow up with clients from the week before 3	Internet marketing blogs and post (few times a week) 4	Call and visit locations for brochures 5	Creative ways to market business 6	7	Add to calendar schedule for the week 8
9	Follow up with clients from the week before 10	Internet marketing blogs and post (few times a week) 11	Find locations for brochures 12	Creative ways to market business 13	Evaluate marketing strategy 14	Add to calendar schedule for the week 15
Look over business plan add to calendar 16	Follow up with clients from the week before 17	Internet marketing blogs and post (few times a week) 18	Find locations for brochures 19	Creative ways to market business 20	21	Add to calendar schedule for the week 22
23	Follow up with clients from the week before 24	Internet marketing blogs and post (few times a week) 25	Find locations for brochures 26	Creative ways to market business 27	Evaluate marketing strategy 28	Add to calendar schedule for the week 29
30	1	2	3	4	5	6

Online Marketing

There are many ways to market your business on the internet. Doing your homework and figuring out what works best for your business goals is important. Here are a few ways to market your business on the internet:

Blogs - A blog can be on your website or can standalone as a blogging website. It is a type of website in which text and pictures can be posted on a regular basis; a conversational style of writing that the public is able to read and comment. Often blogs focus on a particular "area of interest".

A blog is a place where you can share information on anything you want. Using blogs with the right keywords is a great way for people to find you when they are searching for that subject. Blogs are searched out by key words found in the text. Using your selected keywords through blogs gives search engines higher chance for you to come up when people search for the same keywords you have in the blog. Good ideas for blogs are as follows:

- Write blogs weekly pretainding to different aspects of your business.
- Add picture(s) that pertain to the subject in the blog.
- Offer incentives for people to click over to your website.
- Include your name and website so potential clients can to contact you.

Social Networks

Social networks are another way to market yourself. Some popular avenues are Twitter, Instagram, Facebook, Pintrest, Linkedin and any number of the other online services where people can find you. Expand your potential market by writing posts on your social networking pages (blogs) and your website frequently. Doing this often broadens your chances of people seeing your business. Keywords work the same way on social media as it does on search engines. Also, just like blogs it's very important to post different aspects of the business to attract multiple audiences. With social media they make it easier to get your information out to a big audience. Try engaging your audience with a post that makes the reader share with their friends which then increases the impressions (views) of that post.

Search Engine Optimization

The internet is important for building businesses. People often find what they are looking for by typing words in search engines. These words are called keywords. Search engines sends things like "spiders" into the worldwide web and searches for keywords, meta-tags, images, etc. Search engines will then interpret these, and will be able to direct the searcher to a reliable destination. These are all used to draw in potential clients to your website when set up correctly. There are two parts of search engine optimization; organic and pay-per-click.

Paid-Per Section is normally the first few results and sometimes are located on the right side when searching online. They are normally marked with words like "Paid Sponsor." Some people say this is the most effective method of marketing but without enough financial capital it is almost impossible to fight with the expense of keeping your name first.

Organic Section is driven completely on keywords, keywords description, meta-tags, meta-tag descriptions, images, page titles and page descriptions and even more. The best placement is the first few spots on the organic side of search engines. Learning how to get there is a challenge. It takes time to research this position but is reachable when taking the right steps. There are companies that specialize in search engine optimization.

Affiliate Marketing - Affiliate marketing is the process of selling your products or services through a third person/businesses via their website or social media, etc. on a commission basis.

Images - It is important to name the pictures on your website correctly. When people are searching the subject that pertains to your business, the internet recognizes the pictures.

Analytics - Analytics is analyzing how well your website's marketing performance is working. This pertains to keywords and traffic so you can track highly searched words for your website. Knowem.com is one website that helps you find places to blog or post and manage your search engine optimization.

Email - Keeping in contact through email with clients is another great way to say hello and to let them know of upcoming specials or events. There are such companies like Constant Contact and Campaigner that will send out an email flier to all your clients that you can custom design through their website.

Forums - A forum is an online community where potential clients may read and post topics pertaining to their interest. Forums can also be useful for anyone searching for business information, both in terms of reading the content on the subject and actively participating in the discussions.

The Importance of a Website

A website can be your biggest tool while trying to create a lucrative business. The first page is very crucial to the person viewing your website. Today's mindset for an online research/shopper is very quick and judgmental. They want to see what you have to offer and how to get it right away. They also want to know if you are the best choice possible for their new microblade experience.

Your website is basically 2 different functions. Knowing how to master each function and how to draw people to utilizing them is very important.

Here is a descriptions of each one:

Front End: This side is basically everything that your client sees. Pictures with correct names and watermarks can boost up your rankings in the SEO (Search Engine Optimization) world as well as cancel out anyone trying to use your pictures as theirs. The name of a picture and it's descrip-

tion can be used as keywords to give your picture visibility to the public. Watermarks are a mode of security for your pictures. You will need to add keywords to your text to make them searchable.

Back End: This side is mainly about marketing for Search Engine Optimization. Here you will be able to add all your keywords, keywords description, meta-tags, meta tag descriptions, images, page titles and page descriptions.

All these are different ways for the internet to pick up your website on different search engines.

Research the best keywords for microblading because quantity isn't better than quality in this case . Here are some important tips for giving your website the best chance of visibility on search engines and consumers being able to find what they need right away:

- Try and use each of the keywords in almost all of your paragraphs, the first paragraph of your website is the most important.
- Make sure to go back and see which keywords are working for you and which ones are giving negative results.
- Try to display pictures of your best work near the top so your potential clients can see them right away.
- Keep your website clean from clutter, give precise and direct information with "Contact Now" buttons/links available throughout the website.
- Update Reviews/Testimonials as often as possible as they are great tools for helping potential clients feel comfortable.

Clients are Walking Advertisements

When your clients are happy with their eyebrows they will tell their friends about their new found love for microblading. Take the extra steps to make sure you have satisfied clients. There are countless people with whom your clients come in contact with i.e., their friends, relatives, coworkers, etc. The client's hairstylist is usually the first to notice how beautiful their clients new eyebrows look and will often want to have it done themselves. Additionally, they let other clients know about the nice eyebrows they have seen. It is great when your clients show off their eyebrows and tell people how much time they save in the morning. What a wonderful source of word-of-mouth advertising!

Cards and Brochure Information

Take the time to put together an informative brochure with before and after pictures. For more information on before and after pictures see page 17. Adding a picture of yourself can be also beneficial. Potential clients like to see who will be performing their microblading procedure. Your background in the beauty industry or any related field should also be added to your brochure. If you have been a makeup artist, cosmetologist, cosmetician and/or nurse, etc. Let them know. This tells a lot about you and shows that you are taking your career as a microblade artist seriously. Here are a few questions you may want to answer in your brochure:

- Who are microblade clients?
- What types of procedures are available?
- How long does it last?
- Will it look natural?
- How long does it take?
- Is microblading safe?

Booking Appointments on the Phone

How you market yourself when a potential client calls is an important time to start gaining their trust and building a rapport with them. You want to make your clients feel comfortable by letting them know they are making the right choice by selecting you to apply their microblade procedure. Let them know you will be drawing on and measuring the procedure(s) before you begin. When people call, keep a log of how they heard about you. It is always good to keep track of where your business is coming from for future reference. This is important when deciding which marketing efforts seem to be paying off.

Improve Your Consultations

Here are a few tips that can help impress a potential client during their consultation:

- Consider your workspace, is it clean? Is it tidy? Is it noisy? Try to create a spa-like atmosphere for your client so they feel relaxed when they walk through the door. Keep your desk neat and your workspace tidy and clean. Minimize outside distractions and noise. You do not need to have a large space, but make it presentable and professional.

- Start off your consultation by allowing your potential client to browse through your portfolio, brochures and any additional material you may have for them. This will answer many of the questions they may have for you.

- Draw on the procedure(s) your client is considering. Many people think they may want a certain look they are used to, but it may not enhance their facial features or be something they would like in the future. Put your clients best interest first. Don't hesitate to give your expert opinion regarding what you think would enhance their looks.

Beauty Research Industries